D0875862

CONCISE GUIDE TO

Assessment and Management of Violent Patients

American Psychiatric Press
CONCISE GUIDES

Robert E. Hales, M.D.
Series Editor

CONCISE GUIDE TO

Assessment and Management
of Violent Patients

Kenneth Tardiff, M.D., M.P.H.

Cornell Medical College
Department of Psychiatry
Payne Whitney Clinic
New York, New York

American
Psychiatric
Press, Inc.

1400 K Street, N.W.
Washington, DC 20005

89 90 91 92 5 4 3 2 1

The paper used in this publication meets the minimum requirements of the American National Standard for Information Sciences—Permanence of Paper for Printed Library Materials, ANSI Z39.48–1984.   ∞

Library of Congress Cataloging-in-Publication Data

Tardiff, Kenneth, 1944–
    Concise guide to assessment and management of violent patients / Kenneth Tardiff.
        p.   cm. — (Concise guides / American Psychiatric Press)
    Includes bibliographies and index.
    ISBN 0-88048-124-2 (alk. paper)
    1. Violence in psychiatric hospitals—Handbooks, manuals, etc. 2. Violence—Treatment—Handbooks, manuals, etc. I. Title II. Series: Concise guides (American Psychiatric Press)
    [DNLM: 1. Mental Disorders—therapy.
    2. Violence.   WM 100 T183c]
RC439.4.T37   1989
362.2'1—dc19
DNLM/DLC
for Library of Congress   88-36585
                                                              CIP

042193

CONTENTS

INTRODUCTION

to the *American Psychiatric Press Concise Guides*

The *American Psychiatric Press Concise Guides* series provides, in a most accessible format, practical information for psychiatrists—and especially for psychiatry residents and medical students—working in such varied treatment settings as inpatient psychiatry services, outpatient clinics, consultation-liaison services, and private practice. The *Concise Guides* are meant to complement the more detailed information to be found in lengthier psychiatry texts.

The *Concise Guides* address topics of greatest concern to psychiatrists in clinical practice. The books in this series contain a detailed Table of Contents, along with an index, tables, and charts, for easy access; and their size, designed to fit into a lab coat pocket, makes them a convenient source of information. The number of references has been limited to those most relevant to the material presented.

For psychiatrists working in a wide range of clinical situations, understanding the causes of violence and interventions required to manage violent patients is essential. The *Concise Guide to Assessment and Management of Violent Patients* provides psychiatry residents, psychiatrists, and other mental health professionals with important information required to manage potentially violent patients. The author, Dr. Kenneth Tardiff, is a nationally recognized expert in this important clinical area. A member of the faculty at the Cornell University Medical College, Dr. Tardiff has lectured and written extensively about human violence and violent patients. I am particularly pleased that Dr. Tardiff has written this outstanding guide because the issues raised are frequently encountered, especially in inpatient psychiatric units. It is well recognized that younger clinicians are at highest risk for being a victim of violence from a patient; this *Concise Guide* should be required reading for this group. Experienced private practitioners are also not immune from violent acts, and Dr. Tardiff provides helpful information to them in the arrangement of their office environment.

I have read many of Ken Tardiff's articles, monographs, and books on this topic. I believe that the reader will be pleased with the new, up-to-date, and clinically relevant material contained in this *Concise Guide*. He emphasizes throughout the practical and clinically useful material that psychiatrists will need to know in their day-to-day work in general hospitals, private psychiatric hospitals, and outpatient facilities. We all frequently underestimate the potential for human violence in our patients and, when confronted with such situations, may lack the proper answers or fail to take the appropriate action. Dr. Tardiff certainly corrects this potential problem through the publication of the *Concise Guide to Assessment and Management of Violent Patients*. I find myself referring frequently to this wonderful pocket-size book when asked questions by residents on how I would handle potentially violent patients in the emergency room, on the ward, or in an office environment. Readers should find this a helpful addition to their medical library. Dr. Tardiff is congratulated for a job well done.

Robert E. Hales, M.D.
Series Editor
American Psychiatric Press Concise Guides

INTRODUCTION

Violence generates many emotions among clinicians for a number of reasons. For some it is incomprehensible that one human being would deliberately injure another. There is fear for one's own safety or the safety of one's family. There is fear of the ethical and legal ramifications of one's patient injuring or even killing others in society. Furthermore, management of violence is coming under increasing scrutiny through legal processes as well as the written and televised media. Some clinicians have attempted to deal with these emotions and concerns by avoiding treatment situations involving violent patients.

Avoiding violent patients is not an option because the clinician can encounter a violent patient in any treatment setting, private offices and medical units as well as psychiatric inpatient units. This book, intended to equip the clinician to deal with violence in various treatment situations, presents what we know about the causes of violence among psychiatric patients and about the assessment and management of violent patients.

Chapter 2 presents an overview of violence in society and the complex interaction of the characteristics of individuals with influences in the environment. It attempts to place violence among psychiatric patients in perspective in terms of the larger picture of violence in society. Knowledge about the causes of violence is essential for the educated mental health professional as a member of society, but even more importantly for the assessment and planning of treatment for the individual patient.

In Chapter 3 the first contact with the violent patient in the emergency situation is discussed. There is great emphasis on the safety of the clinician and others in terms of whether to attempt to talk to the patient as opposed to using restrictive means of control (e.g., seclusion or involuntary medication). To ensure safety, attention must be given to the physical environment where the interview takes place. Specific practical instructions about physical maneuvers to protect oneself against violence by a patient are presented.

In Chapter 4, two effective means of controlling violent behavior—seclusion and restraint—are presented in detail. These techniques are discussed relative to other means of controlling violent behavior among psychiatric patients (e.g., verbal intervention and the use of emergency medication). Indications and contraindications for seclusion and restraint based on national American Psychiatric Association guidelines are presented. After the decision to seclude or restrain the patient is made, there are basic principles in terms of implementation of seclusion or restraint. The responsibility of the physician is discussed in relation to when the patient should be seen and how often. Responsibility of the nursing staff in terms of monitoring and caring for the patient in seclusion or restraint is then discussed. Last, there are recommendations as to how the staff can determine when the patient is ready to be removed from seclusion or restraint.

The use of emergency medication, particularly rapid neuroleptization, is presented in Chapter 5. The use of low-potency neuroleptic medications versus the use of high-potency neuroleptic medications with concurrent lorazepam (for sedation) is discussed.

Once the emergency has subsided and violence has been controlled, the clinician can proceed with the extended evaluation of the violent patient. Chapter 6 outlines the information that should be obtained from the patient, the family, and others in the structure of the traditional psychiatric interview. In the assessment of the mental status and physical examination, signs and symptoms are discussed in relation to category of disorders associated with violence, including organic disorders, psychoactive substances, other substances, primary diseases of the brain associated with violence, systemic disorders associated with violence, schizophrenia, delusional (paranoid) disorder, mood disorders, personality disorders, mental retardation, and disruptive behavior disorders.

Once the patient has been properly evaluated and the diagnosis has been established, the use of the appropriate long-term medication must be considered. The indications, dosages, and side effects of a number of medications (i.e., neuroleptics, anxiolytic drugs and sedatives, carbamazepine and other anticonvulsants, propranolol, lithium, psychostimulants, and tryptophan) are discussed in Chapter 7.

In Chapter 8, the long-term psychotherapy of violent patients with or without long-term medication is discussed. It is important that the clinician know which types of violent patients are amenable to long-term psychotherapy and to define clearly the goals of psychotherapy, including evaluating the motivation of the patient, helping the patient achieve self-control, dealing with transference and countertransference, fostering the development of insight and emotional awareness, and increasing the patient's ability to appreciate the consequences of violence. The safety of the therapist in the outpatient setting is discussed in terms of transference and countertransference, threats from patients, and the physical characteristics of the office setting.

In Chapter 9, behavioral therapy is presented, not to equip the clinician to plan and implement such a treatment program, but to give the clinician an appreciation of the power of this technique of managing violent behavior.

In Chapter 10, a model for the short-term prediction of violence analogous to the assessment of suicide potential is presented. Although this model should be subjected to further research, it can serve as a standard of what information should be considered in determining whether a patient poses a risk of violence to others within a matter of days or at most a week. The need to document the fact that the clinician has gathered these data and used them in a logical manner to form a decision about violence is emphasized.

In Chapter 11, legal issues related to the management of violent patients are discussed in terms of principles and not specific case decisions, which may vary across jurisdictions. The basic ethical and legal principles that balance the liberty of the individual in relation to deprivation of liberty to protect the individual from himself or herself or to protect others in society is discussed. Basic legal principles involved with involuntary hospitalization, informed consent, involuntary treatment, seclusion and restraint, and the clinician's duty to protect others are presented.

I hope that this book will serve as a basic handbook and allay the fears and concerns of clinicians when they encounter violent patients. This brief guide is not meant to be all-inclusive in terms of what is known about the evaluation and management of violence among psychiatric patients and is not meant to dissuade further research on violence among psychiatric patients.

2 CAUSES OF HUMAN VIOLENCE

In this chapter I will review a spectrum of studies aimed at determining why some people manifest violent behavior toward others. The goal is to present possible etiologic factors that, of course, would be related to the evaluation, treatment, and, it is hoped, prevention of human violence. In considering the causes of human violence, one must use a multifactorial model. One may conceptualize a group of factors within the individual as increasing or decreasing that individual's predisposition to violence. These factors may be present at the time of birth or may be acquired during childhood development. These internal factors interact with external factors, which may tip the balance toward violent behavior.

■ NEUROPHYSIOLOGIC FACTORS

In the search for a biologic basis for violent behavior, researchers have explored the limbic system of the brain. Building on a number of their own previous studies and studies done by others, Mark and Ervin (1) and Monroe (2) called attention to the role of neurophysiologic dysfunction of the brain; the former investigator in terms of temporal lobe epilepsy (now called partial complex seizures), and the latter investigator in a more subtle sense, that of limbic ictus and episodic dyscontrol.

A decade later, a large international collaborative study of violence, defined as "directed exertion of extreme and aggressive physical force which, if unrestrained, would result in injury, destruction or abuse," found that significant violence was rare among epileptic patients during seizures (3). Furthermore, aggressive behavior during seizures was usually stereotyped, unsustained, and not purposeful in nature. Leicester (4) looked at 500 cases referred to a neurologist and found that of the 17 patients referred for temper tantrums, none had organic factors (i.e., epilepsy or episodic dyscontrol syndrome). Rather, the violent episodes were the results of psychological factors. Finally, Hermann and Whitman (5) reviewed 64 studies conducted since 1962 that assessed the relation among temporal lobe epilepsy, aggression, and other forms of psychopathology. They focused on studies of the interictal period in terms of irritable, aggressive, or hostile behavior using neurosurgical and nonneurosurgical patients, as well as surveys of prison populations. They concluded that controlled investigations showed no overall differences in the levels of violence between persons with and without epilepsy. Among individuals with epilepsy, other factors were found to be associated with violence per se (e.g., low socioeconomic status, sex, age, problems with the earlier development of the individual).

Lewis et al. (6) found that of 97 delinquent adolescent boys in correctional schools, 18 had psychomotor epilepsy, and that the more violent boys were those with this disorder. Five boys committed violent acts during seizures, but violence was interictal as well. The violent boys with temporal lobe epilepsy were more likely to report impaired or distorted memory and to have low IQs, a frequent history of head trauma, and paranoid ideation or hallucinations, all of which were associated with poor impulse control and were not directly related to seizures. Thus the individual may manifest violence secondary to seizure activity on one occasion and as a result of other factors associated with poor impulse control on other occasions.

Devinsky and Baer (7) have continued to emphasize the importance of temporal lobe epilepsy in violence and have illustrated various forms of violence that one may encounter through the use of case histories. They did not address the prevalence of violent behavior among temporal lobe epileptic patients compared to the general epileptic population or to the general nonepileptic population. They did criticize studies that used patients with generalized seizures in control groups because a primary limbic focus may be obscured by general seizure activity or a secondary limbic focus of the seizure activity may result from the generalized seizure activity. Likewise, Monroe (8) has continued to maintain that episodic dyscontrol is often associated with limbic ictus but is not detected because the surface electroencephalogram is an insensitive procedure for measuring subcortical activity. He pointed out that support for his theory of limbic ictal phenomena rests with the response of individuals with dyscontrol to anticonvulsant regimens.

■ NEUROTRANSMITTERS

Earlier studies of neurotransmitters have implicated increased levels of norepinephrine and dopamine in aggressive behavior (9). Others have implicated the serotonergic system. Brown et al. (10, 11) conducted two studies of men with a history of aggressive behavior, excluding those with a history of primary affective disorders, schizophrenia, or severe brain syndromes, as well as those ingesting drugs or alcohol 10 days preceding the study. They found that a history of aggressive behavior and a history of suicidal behavior were related to decreased cerebrospinal fluid (CSF) 5-hydroxyindoleacetic acid (5-HIAA) levels. They believe that altered serotonin metabolism may be a highly significant contributing factor to these behaviors in whatever diagnostic group they occur. Lidberg et al. (12) studied the CSF 5-HIAA levels in a group of men convicted of criminal homicide and a group of men who attempted suicide, and found that these groups had lower levels of 5-HIAA in CSF than did male controls. They did not, as Brown et al. did, exclude alcoholics or patients with schizophrenia or affective illness. Linnolia et al. (13) studied violent offenders, excluding schizophrenics or those with major affective disorders, but not alcoholics. All of the subjects had killed or attempted to kill with unusual cruelty. They found that impulsive offenders had significantly lower CSF 5-HIAA concentrations than nonimpulsive offenders, the latter group defined as those who had premeditated their crimes. Furthermore, those offenders with a history of suicide attempts had lower CSF 5-HIAA concentration levels than those without a history of suicide. Thus low CSF 5-HIAA concentration may be a marker of impulsivity rather than of a specific type of violence.

■ GENETICS

In terms of specific genetic defects, there has been interest and research over the past two decades in sex chromosome abnormalities. A link with specific genetic abnormalities and homicide and other acts of violence would be important in terms of criminal responsibility. There have been a number of surveys of men in prisons and other correctional institutions showing that XYY men are disproportionately represented. Some studies have attempted to eliminate the sampling bias inherent in obtaining subjects from the institutionalized population. Schiavi et al. (14) reviewed the literature and conducted a double-blind controlled study in Copenhagen. They found no association between the

XYY or XXY chromosomal abnormalities and violence. It appears that the specific role of these sex chromosome abnormalities is doubtful and that any association with arrests for crimes is probably linked to other factors (e.g., the low intelligence of these men).

There is some evidence that genetic inheritance is related to criminal acts. Mednick and Volavka (15) pointed out that earlier twin studies showing increased criminal behavior in monozygotic twins as compared to dizygotic twins were subject to a number of sampling problems; however, more recent studies using better methodology also have found increased criminal behavior in monozygotic as compared to dizygotic twins. Given that twins share the same environmental as well as genetic backgrounds, further investigation has turned to adoption studies. Bohman et al. (16) reported that a study of adopted men in Sweden committing violent crimes showed that their crimes were related to their own alcohol abuse, but not to violence in their biologic or adoptive parents, although nonviolent petty property crime did seem to have a genetic predisposition.

In summary, there appears to be no specific chromosomal abnormality that accounts for violent behavior. Studies of inheritance support only a genetic relationship for economic, property crimes, not for violence.

■ PSYCHIATRIC DISORDERS

Although many acts of violence, particularly those related to economic motives, are not committed by psychiatric patients, the role of psychiatric disorders in violent behavior had been a subject of study for decades. In his review of a number of studies, Rabkin (17) concluded that arrest and conviction rates for violent crimes among psychiatric patients exceed those for the general population and that there has been a pronounced relative as well as absolute increase in these rates over time. This increase in rates may be related to policies that have increasingly discharged patients into the community.

Yet psychiatric patients should not be regarded as a homogeneous group. Tardiff and Sweillam (18–20) found that violent patients admitted to and residing in both public and private hospitals are more likely than nonviolent patients to have diagnoses of schizophrenia, mania, mental retardation, and organic mental disorders. Taylor (21) examined 203 male prisoners and found that 46 percent were directly driven to commit violent offenses by their psychotic symptoms and, if indirect consequences of the psychosis were taken into account, 82 percent of their offenses were probably attributable to their illness. Within the psychotic group, those driven to offend by their delusions were more likely to have been seriously violent. A review of the literature including these and other studies of violence among psychiatric inpatients confirmed that diagnosis and course of the illness are important factors in predicting the incidence of violence in hospitals (22).

However, if one looks at a different treatment setting—the outpatient clinic rather than the inpatient psychiatry unit or prison—psychiatric patients with increased rates of assault do not have psychotic diagnoses, but rather have diagnoses of childhood, adolescent, and personality disorders (23).

Menuck (24) reviewed the literature on some of these personality disorders, including the borderline as well as the overcontrolled types of personality disorders. In addition, he reviewed studies relating violence to alcohol, with its concurrent releasing of inhibitions against antisocial and violent behavior and decreasing perceptual and cognitive alertness with resulting impairment of judgment. There are a number of epidemiologic studies that have found a strong link between alcohol use and certain types of homicide involving disputes (25, 26). A number of street drugs of abuse (e.g., amphetamines, cocaine, hallucinogens, minor tranquilizers-sedatives) have been found to be associated with violent behavior (24, 27). In a study of homicides in Manhattan, opiate drug abuse was related to violence indirectly and not in terms of a primary psychopharmacologic effect (26). Narcotics played a key role because of the activities aimed at obtaining these drugs. One-third of male homicide victims died in drug-related homicides.

■ DEVELOPMENTAL FACTORS

Some factors impact on the development of the individual and shift the balance of one's character toward violence as an adult. Kempe and Helfer (28) reported that being abused as a child is related to becoming a physically abusive adult (i.e., a child abuser or otherwise violent adult). There is also evidence that witnessing intrafamily violence (e.g., spouse abuse) is related to increased problems with violence among children, especially boys (e.g., hyperactivity, cruelty, bullying, and temper tantrums) (29).

We see that child and spouse abuse are significant problems in the United States, and that being abused as a child or being in a family where a spouse is abused tips the balance toward being violent as an adult. Of course, child and domestic violence is not a primary cause of adult violence, but is in a chain of causation. Other characteristics of the child that are important in child abuse include being premature, being a sick child, or demonstrating behavior or having a physical appearance that generates a violent reaction by the parent because of the parent's own psychopathology (28).

■ SOCIOECONOMIC FACTORS

There have been a number of studies that have attempted to dissect the factors of race, culture, and economics in the production of violence in society. Criminal violence in black ghettos has been explained in terms of the necessity to fight rather than break up families, alienation, discrimination, and frustration. Thus some have hypothesized that blacks live in a violent subculture (30); others have found that there is no difference between blacks and whites in domestic violence if socioeconomic status is controlled in the analysis (31).

In a study of large standard metropolitan statistical areas that compared rates of violent crime, including homicide as reported by the Federal Bureau of Investigation, Blau and Blau (32) found that racial inequality and stress were associated with rates of homicides. Economic inequality was not merely poverty, but rather relative to other persons. Some studies found that absolute poverty is related to violence and other criminal behavior (33).

The contradictory results are probably due to the use of large metropolitan areas as units of analysis. A study by Messner and Tardiff (34) used neighborhoods as smaller units of analysis, which were more naturalistic, to test the hypothesis that economic inequality is related to homicide. They found that economic inequality and race were not related to homicide, but rather that the prime determinants were absolute poverty and marital disruption.

Thus the social determinants of violence are linked in a cycle in terms of 1) poverty and the inability to have basic necessities of life; 2) disruption of marriages; 3) production of single-parent families; 4) unemployment; and 5) further difficulty in maintaining interpersonal ties, family structures, and social control.

■ OTHER ENVIRONMENTAL FACTORS

Physical crowding seems to be related to violent crime. Some contend that there is increased contact, decreased defensible space, and increased violence in high-density areas; others argue that increased density is related to increased social control and decreased violent crime. Bell and Baron (35) reviewed a number of ecologic and ethnologic studies as well as laboratory studies that correlated the ambient temperature of the environment with violent crime and riots. They concluded that there is a relation between heat and aggression that is curvilinear: moderately uncomfortable ambient temperatures produce an increase of aggression, whereas extremely hot temperatures decrease aggression and lead to flight rather than fight.

The clinician should appreciate the social and economic setting in which the violent patient lives for purposes of evaluation and treatment. Furthermore, the environmental determinants of violence in society (e.g., overcrowding, heat, the role of others around the potentially violent individual) have direct relevance to violence by patients in an inpatient hospital setting. Inpatient violence is affected by the number of patients in relation to the number of staff on the unit, as well as to the education, experience, and attitudes of the staff. Patients must have the opportunity to participate in their environment and to interact with staff members and other patients if isolation, anger, and violence are to be avoided.

■ CONCLUSION

Violence is the result of a complex interaction of the characteristics of the individual with influences in the environment. As is seen in Table 1, biologic or innate predisposing factors such as neurophysiologic dysfunction, inheritance, neurotransmitter abnormalities, or certain psychiatric disorders are nonspecific in the way they cause violence. Rather than a specific mechanism, they tip the balance by impairing the individual's ability to achieve goals by more appropriate nonviolent means or by increasing impulsivity, irritability, irrationality, or disorganization of behavior.

The influence of the environment around the individual exerts its effects during development of the individual and more immediately preceding the violent episode. Influences during development include having been subjected to physical abuse as a child or witnessing violence within one's family or subculture. Environmental factors that precede the violent episode include the setting of poverty and other adverse social conditions that have a damaging effect on the individual, the family, and the

TABLE 1. **Research on Causes of Human Violence**

1. **Innate Factors**
   Partial complex seizures
   Subtle neurophysiologic dysfunction secondary to head trauma, etc.
   Increased norepinephrine and dopamine
   Decreased serotonin and impulsivity
   Genetic inheritance versus chromosomal abnormalities
   Psychosis and other psychopathology
   Alcohol and drug abuse

2. **Developmental Factors**
   Physical abuse as a child
   Witnessing domestic violence
   Portrayal of violence in mass media

3. **Socioeconomic Factors**
   Subcultures
   Racial inequality
   Economic inequality
   Absolute poverty
   Marital and familial disruption

4. **Physical Environment**
   Crowding
   Heat

social network as well as the more immediate influence of alcohol and drug abuse.

Although this chapter is merely a brief overview of the causes of violence, numerous references to the scientific literature are listed so as to allow the clinician to read further in this area. Understanding the roots of violence is of great importance. For the individual patient, some biologic and environmental factors may be more important than others, but it is the responsibility of the clinician to weigh all of these in the evaluation of the individual, in the determination of the danger he or she poses to others, and in the planning and implementation of treatment. These factors are dealt with more specifically throughout this book.

Even if the assessment and treatment of violent patients did not demand knowledge of the causes of violence, the clinician should feel obliged to read further about the causes of violence as an informed member of society.

■ REFERENCES

1. Mark VH, Ervin FR: Violence and the Brain. New York, Harper and Row, 1970
2. Monroe RR: Episodic Behavioral Disorders. Cambridge, Harvard University Press, 1970
3. Delgado-Escueta AV, Mattson RH, King L, et al: The nature of aggression during epileptic seizures. N Engl J Med 1981; 305: 711–716
4. Leicester J: Temper tantrums, epilepsy and episodic dyscontrol. Br J Psychiatry 1982; 141:262–266
5. Hermann BP, Whitman S: Behavioral and personality correlates of epilepsy: a review, methodological critique and conceptual model. Psychol Bull 1984; 95:451–497
6. Lewis DO, Pincus JH, Shanok SS, et al: Psychomotor epilepsy and violence in a group of incarcerated adolescent boys. Am J Psychiatry 1982; 139:882–886
7. Devinsky O, Baer D: Varieties of aggressive behavior in temporal lobe epilepsy. Am J Psychiatry 1984; 141:651–656
8. Monroe RR: Episodic behavioral disorders and limbic ictus. Compr Psychiatry 1985; 26:466–479
9. Eichelman B, Elliott GR, Barchas J: Biomedical, pharmacological and genetic aspects of aggression, in Behavioral Aspects of Aggression. Edited by Hamburg DA, Trudeau MB. New York, Alan R Liss, 1981

10. Brown GL, Goodwin FK, Ballenger JC, et al: Aggression in humans correlates with cerebrospinal fluid amine metabolites. Psychiatry Res 1979; 1:131–139

11. Brown GL, Ebert MH, Goyer PF, et al: Aggression, suicide and serotonin: relationship to CSF amine metabolites. Am J Psychiatry 1982; 136:741–746

12. Lidberg L, Tuck JR, Asberg M, et al: Homicide, suicide and CSF 5-HIAA. Acta Psychiatr Scand 1985; 71:230–236

13. Linnolia M, Virkkunen M, Scheinin M, et al: Low cerebrospinal fluid 5-hydroxyindoleacetic acid concentration differentiates impulsive from nonimpulsive violent behavior. Life Sci 1983; 33:2609–2614

14. Schiavi RC, Theilgaard A, Owen DR, et al: Sex chromosome abnormalities, hormones and aggressivity. Arch Gen Psychiatry 1984: 41:93–99

15. Mednick SA, Volavka J: Biology and crime, in Crime and Justice: An Annual Review of Research, vol 2. Edited by Morris N, Touny M. Chicago, University of Chicago Press, 1980

16. Bohman M, Cloninger R, Sigvardsson S, et al: Predisposition to petty criminality in Swedish adoptees. Arch Gen Psychiatry 1982; 39: 1233–1241

17. Rabkin JG: Criminal behavior of discharged mental patients: a critical review of the research. Psychol Bull 1979; 86:1–27

18. Tardiff K, Sweillam A: Assault, suicide and mental illness. Arch Gen Psychiatry 1980; 37:164–169

19. Tardiff K, Sweillam A: The occurrence of assaultive behavior among chronic psychiatric inpatients. Am J Psychiatry 1982; 139:212–215

20. Tardiff K, Sweillam A: Characteristics of assaultive patients in private psychiatric hospitals. Am J Psychiatry 1984; 141:1232–1235

21. Taylor PJ: Motives for offending among violent and psychotic men. Br J Psychiatry 1985; 147:491–498

22. Krakowski M, Volavka J, Brizer D: Psychopathology and violence: a review of the literature. Compr Psychiatry 1986; 27:131–148

23. Tardiff K, Koenigsberg HW: Assaultive behavior among psychiatric outpatients. Am J Psychiatry 1985; 142:960–963

24. Menuck M: Clinical aspects of dangerous behavior. Journal of Psychiatry and Law 1983; 11:227–304

25. Goodman RA, Mercy JA, Loya F, et al: Alcohol use and interpersonal violence: alcohol detected in homicide victims. Am J Public Health 1986; 76:144–149

26. Tardiff K, Gross E, Messner S: A study of homicide in Manhattan, 1981. Am J Public Health 1986; 76:139–143

27. Nurco, DN, Ball JC, Shaffer JW, et al: The criminality of narcotic addicts. J Nerv Ment Dis 1985; 173:94–102

28. Kempe CH, Helfer R (eds): The Battered Child Syndrome, 3rd ed. Chicago, University of Chicago Press, 1980

29. Jaffe P, Wolfe D, Wilson SK, et al: Family violence and child adjustment: a comparative analysis of girls' and boys' behavioral symptoms. Am J Psychiatry 1986; 143:74–77

30. Wolfgang ME: Sociocultural overview of criminal violence, in Violence and the Violent Individual. Edited by Hays JR, Roberts TK, Solway KS. New York, SP Medical and Scientific Publications, 1981

31. Centerwall BS: Race, socioeconomic status and domestic homicide: Atlanta, 1971–72. Am J Public Health 1984; 74:813–815

32. Blau JR, Blau PM: The cost of inequality: metropolitan structure and violent crime. American Sociological Review 1982; 47:114–129

33. Williams K: Economic sources of homicide: reestimating the effects of poverty and inequality. American Sociological Review 1984; 49:283–289

34. Messner S, Tardiff K: Economic inequality and levels of homicide: an analysis of urban neighborhoods. Criminology 1986; 24:297–317

35. Bell PA, Baron RA: Ambient temperature and human violence, in Multidisciplinary Approaches to Aggression Research. Edited by Brain PF, Benton D. Amsterdam, Elsevier/North Holland, 1981

3 FIRST CONTACT WITH ACUTELY VIOLENT PATIENTS

■ SAFETY FIRST

Most clinicians will recall the first encounter with a violent patient in the emergency room, the inpatient unit, or the outpatient clinic where the patient has just struck someone, thrown something, or threatened violence. There may be a group of people around the patient: staff, police, patients, and other observers. The psychiatrist or other clinician in charge in that setting is expected to handle the situation. The foremost thought in the clinician's mind at that point should be safety. The clinician must feel safe with the patient or else it will interfere with the evaluation and may result in physical injury or death. Thought should be given to self-defense in the emergency situation.

■ TO TALK OR NOT TO TALK AND WHERE?

In emergency situations, the clinician must decide what is the best setting in which to interview the patient. A wide range of options should be considered. The most private one is to be with the patient with the door to the office closed. The clinician should sit between the patient and the door in case escape is necessary. The next option is to interview the patient alone in an office with the door open. Next is to interview the patient in the office with the door open and the staff outside the door. The next option is to interview the patient in an office with staff present. The most extreme option is to interview the patient while the patient is in physical restraints. The clinician should not feel omnipotent despite the thought that others expect the clinician to have magical powers in calming violent patients. In addition to relying on one's feelings concerning safety, one should take into consideration the possibility of countertransference reactions or other inappropriate reactions (e.g., denial) that will interfere with the effective management of a particular patient. This will be discussed at length later in Chapters 4 and 8.

In deciding how to proceed in terms of talking to the patient or using physical means of control, one should make an instant differential diagnosis and categorize the patient into one of three groups:

1. *Organic mental disorder:* In this group, it is often impossible to intervene and influence the patient effectively through verbal means. One should treat the underlying medical or other physical disorder rather than only rely on neuroleptics to control violence. If the etiology is unknown, the patient probably should be restrained as the laboratory tests and evaluation proceed if there is actual violence or imminent violence.
2. *Functional psychosis:* The violent patients in this group are usually schizophrenic or manic and are difficult to influence through verbal means. Neuroleptic medication rapidly administered is usually the treatment of choice for these patients, although the patients may have to be restrained or secluded until it takes effect.
3. *Nonpsychotic, nonorganic disorders:* This group primarily includes patients with personality disorders who are often ame-

nable to verbal intervention without seclusion or restraint. One may want to offer medication to a patient in this group and give the patient the option of either accepting or rejecting the medication, thus giving the patient a sense of control in the situation. In deciding to use physical means of control, the clinician can assess the patient's degree of impulse control by the patient's compliance with routine requests and procedures in the clinic or emergency room.

The use of other means of controlling violence by patients in an emergency situation is discussed in depth in Chapter 4 (i.e., the use of seclusion and restraint) and in Chapter 5 (i.e., the use of emergency medication).

■ TALKING WITH THE VIOLENT PATIENT

If the clinician decides to use verbal techniques to intervene in the emergency situation without physical controls, the following should be borne in mind. The clinician should approach the patient in a calm manner, with the appearance of being in control. The clinician should speak softly in a nonprovocative, nonjudgmental manner and begin by commenting in a neutral concrete manner about the obvious (e.g., "You look angry"). Emotional or pejorative comments (e.g., "Why the hell did you do that?" or "Why don't you act like an adult?") should not be used; they are provocative and will probably result in further violence. There should be adequate space between the clinician and the patient, and both should be sitting. It is important that the clinician not tower over the patient or be intimidating in any way. Respect for the patient should be shown. It is recommended that the clinician avoid continued direct eye contact with the patient; this may be interpreted as being challenging. The clinician should attempt to project a state of passivity, yet a sense of being in control of the situation.

When the patient begins to talk, the clinician should listen and appear empathic, concerned, and uncritical. It is important that the clinician not interrupt the patient; often patients with personality disorders manifesting violence have difficulty in expressing their concerns verbally. The initial phase is not the time for interpretations or attempts at psychodynamic formulations or insights. This may result in provocation and an argument with the patient. The clinician should try to obtain the patient's view of the situation and what led up to the violent episode. Once this has been elicited, the clinician may subtly and gently attempt to state his or her perception of what the situation is and attempt to correct a misperception by the patient. The clinician should not promise something that may not be possible. For example, in the emergency room, the clinician should not promise not to admit the patient to the hospital; on an inpatient unit, the clinician should not promise not to restrict the patient to his or her room or to put the patient into seclusion. The clinician may want to offer the patient medication because it gives the patient a sense of control as to whether it is accepted or rejected. These principles of verbal intervention are summarized in Table 1.

■ INTERVIEWING AND THE PHYSICAL ENVIRONMENT

The clinician should consider the physical aspects of the office or other setting in which violent patients will be interviewed. There should be solid heavy furniture that would be difficult to move or throw. On the other hand, a light chair that could be used as a shield in cases of attack, particularly with sharp weapons, may be advisable. I prefer to sit between the patient and the door. Ideally, there should be two exits so that the

TABLE 1. **Verbal Intervention in Emergencies**

- Present a calm appearance
- Speak softly
- Speak in nonprovocative and nonjudgmental manner
- Speak in neutral, concrete manner
- Put space between yourself and the patient
- Show respect for the patient
- Avoid intense direct eye contact
- Balance your control versus an authoritarian stance
- Facilitate the patient's talking
- Listen to the patient
- Avoid early interpretations
- Do not make promises you cannot keep

clinician may exit if the patient enters the reception area with a weapon. In the clinician's office, there should be no heavy objects such as ashtrays that can be thrown; rather, pillows or other soft objects to use as shields are useful in case of attack. There should be a method for the clinician to indicate that he or she is in danger. This may be in the form of a "panic button" or in a prearranged message such as "please cancel my appointment for . . ." (a time later in the day). Likewise, there should be some way for the receptionist or person outside of the office to indicate a potentially dangerous situation to the clinician before the patient enters the office.

Last, when interviewing patients who have been violent or who are potentially explosive, the clinician should pay attention to his or her dress. Glasses should be removed before interviewing such patients and, in the case of men, one's necktie may be removed or tucked in the shirt. In the case of women, jewelry such as necklaces and earrings should be removed. Likewise, if the patient has been violent and is to be put into seclusion, proper attention should be paid to removing from the patient dangerous clothing (e.g., belts, neckties) and dangerous objects (e.g., pens, jewelry, matches). In fact, in a number of emergency rooms, metal detectors are in place so as to detect weapons and other potentially dangerous items before the patient is seen.

■ PHYSICAL MANEUVERS BY THE CLINICIAN

There are a number of physical maneuvers that should be helpful in preventing or managing attacks by patients (1). When standing, the clinician should not face the patient but turn sideways, preferably with the arms folded or with one arm across the stomach and the other around the chin. In both cases, the clinician should be ready for rapid protective movements with the arms and hands. The clinician must anticipate a punch, a kick, or other attack. The response to the attack depends on the target. For example, the face may be protected with the hands, or a punch may be deflected with the palms of the hands. If deflection is unsuccessful, the clinician should be able to avoid the force of the punch by tucking the head and covering the ears. Thus sensitive areas of the head and throat are protected. A kick should be deflected with the clinician's legs rather than allow it to strike the groin or abdomen. If the clinician has fallen to the floor, feet should be kept toward the patient so as to block kicks by the patient with the feet.

If a weapon such as a knife is produced by the patient, an object such as a chair or clipboard should be used for protection as a shield. If the patient is known to have a weapon such as a knife or piece of glass, staff should be summoned to subdue the patient if a verbal request for the weapon is not followed. A mattress can be used to pin the patient against the wall by four staff members while two of the staff members secure the patient's arms and subsequently disarm the patient. If no objects are available to serve as shields, the clinician should employ the same type of deflections and blocking maneuvers described previously. This may result in injury but may make the difference between survival and death.

If the patient attempts to grab the clinician's wrists, the same deflective movements should be used as are used for punching. If the patient grabs the wrist, the clinician may attempt verbal intervention (e.g., asking the patient to let go). If the clinician has to use physical maneuvers to escape, the clinician's arms should be bent at the elbow and quickly twisted in a circular movement against the patient's thumbs. If grabbed by both wrists from the rear, the clinician should turn under the patient's arm very rapidly and throw the patient off balance and escape. In cases where the hair has been grabbed, the basic principle is to establish immediate control over the patient's hand with the clinician's hands. Once this has been done, further pulling and damage is minimized and further intervention would involve verbal statements or physical attempts to free oneself from the patient's hands. As with other grabbing by the patient, the thumb is often the most vulnerable point in freeing oneself.

If the patient is successful in obtaining a choke hold on the clinician, the basic principle is for the clinician to tuck the chin downward as close to the chest as possible. This flexes the neck muscles and protects critical air and blood circulation structures. This prevents loss of consciousness, and gives the clinician time to escape. If the patient is facing the clinician with a choke hold, the arms should be raised and turned using them as leverage. If the patient is choking the clinician from the rear, again the head should be tucked, and the clinician should turn, using the arms as levers to break the hold. If the patient has the clinician in a headlock, again the chin should be tucked while the head is pulled downward, with both arms pushing the patient's arm upward.

If the patient is biting, rather than attempt to pull the bitten part from the patient's mouth, the clinician should force the part (e.g., an arm) into the patient's mouth further while closing the patient's nostrils, preventing breathing. The arm or other body part can then be withdrawn when the patient takes a breath of air. The basic elements necessary to ensure the safety of the clinician in emergencies are summarized in Table 2.

■ FIREARMS AND HOSTAGE SITUATIONS

If the patient appears in a treatment setting with a weapon (e.g., a gun) there should be exposure of as few staff as possible. For example, if a psychiatrist is aware of such a patient in the reception area, there should be an immediate retreat to the office rather than engaging the patient in the reception area. As many staff as possible should be removed from the treatment area where the patient appears with the gun. The first few minutes in this scenario are crucial. If trapped, the clinician should acknowledge the patient with something obvious (e.g., "I see you have a gun"). The clinician should appear calm and should not be intimidating, confrontational, obnoxious, or argumentative. The clinician should encourage the patient to talk during the initial phases and to repeat the patient's concerns. There should be no attempt to take the weapon from the patient. A suggestion may be made that the patient put the weapon down on a desk. One should not reach for the gun or tell the patient to drop the gun; this could result in discharge of the weapon.

Attention should be given beforehand to ways of warning persons outside of the room that the clinician is in danger. This may be achieved by a panic button that alerts staff in a central location or by some prearranged message on the telephone in which a receptionist outside of the office can be alerted that a dangerous situation exists. There should be a specific written plan as to a course of action (e.g., alerting the police, clearing the area of patients and staff). If the hostage situation continues, obviously this calls for a professional hostage negotiator. The staff person(s)

TABLE 2. **Safety of the Clinician in Emergencies**

1. **Setting of the Interview**
   - Alone in office with door closed
   - Alone in office with door open
   - Alone in office with staff outside
   - In office with staff present
   - With patient in restraints
2. **Analyze Countertransference and Reactions to Patient**
   - Denial
   - Reaction formation
   - Displacement
3. **Instant Differential Diagnosis**
   - Organic mental disorders
     Determine and treat underlying medical disorder and question
     use of verbal intervention
   - Functional psychosis (schizophrenia and mania)
     Neuroleptic medication and question use of verbal intervention
   - Nonpsychotic, nonorganic disorders (primarily personality
     disorders)
     Consider verbal intervention
4. **Physical Environment of the Office**
   - Solid furniture difficult to move
   - Light chair for a shield
   - Sit between patient and the door
   - Two exits are ideal (although rarely available)
   - No ashtrays or other heavy objects
   - Pillows and other soft objects useful
   - "Panic button" or prearranged message to the outside
   - Receptionist should be able to warn clinician of danger
5. **Dress**
   - Remove eyeglasses
   - Tuck in tie
   - Remove jewelry (e.g., necklaces and earrings)
   - Search patient for dangerous items in emergency room
6. **Physical Defense**
   - Stand sideways, not facing the patient
   - Arms ready for defense
   - Deflect kicks with the legs
   - Use office objects as shield for sharp weapons
   - Use mattress as shield for sharp objects on inpatient units
   - Use force against patient's thumb if grabbed
   - Control patient's hand if hair is grabbed
   - Tuck chin rapidly if a choke hold is attempted by the patient

with the patient as the hostage-taking situation continues should attempt to build a rapport with the patient. Hostages who are regarded as people rather than faceless targets are more likely to survive. Turner (2) made specific recommendations concerning such situations. He advised that one do exactly as the hostage taker says and avoid an open display of despair or loss of control (e.g., crying or begging). Hostages should remain observant. In cases where there were a number of hostages, the hostage killed was often the one who behaved in a manner different from the rest. One should not attempt to escape or overpower the hostage taker unless absolutely certain of success. Suggestions on how to deal with this infrequent but life-or-death situation are summarized in Table 3.

TABLE 3. **Dealing with the Patient Who Has a Gun**

- Expose as few staff as possible
- Keep a calm appearance
- Encourage patient to talk and build rapport with the patient
- Suggest that the patient put the gun down
- Do not reach for the gun
- Have a written, known plan for hostage situations

■ REFERENCES

1. Thackrey M: Therapeutics for Aggression: Psychological/Physical Crisis Intervention. New York, Human Sciences Press, 1987
2. Turner JT (ed): Violence in the Medical Care Setting: A Survival Guide. Rockville, Md, Aspen Systems Corp, 1984

SECLUSION AND RESTRAINT 4

■ PREVENTION OF INAPPROPRIATE SECLUSION OR RESTRAINT

Before using seclusion or restraint, verbal intervention should be considered, along the lines discussed in the preceding chapter. In the emergency situation, the staff should be adequate and trained to implement seclusion and restraint techniques effectively, appropriately, and safely. The staff should be caring and nonauthoritarian, yet at the same time be in control of the patient's behavior. Attention should be given to preventing violence by being able to talk with and listen to the patient. The staff should talk to the patient in a calm, nonprovocative manner. As tension increases before violence occurs, even a psychotic schizophrenic patient may respond to nonprovocative interpersonal contact and expression of concern and caring. It is important that the staff recognize the warning signs of violence for an individual patient that have preceded violence in the past. A patient may have manifested a specific pattern of behavior or speech before an explosive episode (e.g., pacing in front of the nursing station).

To prevent inappropriate seclusion or restraint or not using these techniques when they should be used, the staff should know their own feelings about violent patients based on countertransference reactions or other emotional reactions to patients (1). As in other areas of psychiatry, negative or inappropriate feelings about patients must be recognized so as not to act on them. The staff should be constantly monitoring the ward dynamics, particularly in terms of staff conflict, which may translate into inappropriate patient care in the management of violence. The staff should know their own past experiences with violence and how these may affect their treatment of patients. Anger toward a patient for a particular act may be justified or it may be the result of a countertransference where the patient resembles a

The author would like to acknowledge the contribution of the members and consultants of the Task Force consisting of Doctors Donald Gair, Thomas Gutheil, Timothy Kuehnel, Robert Liberman, John Lion, Marlin Mattson, Katherine Slama, Paul Soloff, Manoel Straker, Stephen Wong, and Mr. David Wexler.

significant person from one's past. A number of defense mechanisms may interfere with the treatment of violent patients and may pose a danger to the therapist and others. Denial of a patient's dangerousness may occur because of the therapist's past experiences with violence or because the patient may be particularly attractive or interesting. On the other hand, a patient may be viewed as more dangerous than he or she actually is because of staff anxiety that is projected onto the patient. Displacement can occur from one patient who is dangerous to another who is not dangerous but who serves as an acceptable scapegoat for a staff member. Negative reactions to patients on the basis of bias or prejudice are not acceptable. In addition, ward dynamics may result in the inappropriate treatment of violent patients. For example, the staff may feel abandoned by the administration, or the psychiatrist may inappropriately seclude or restrain a particular patient so as to activate procedures where the psychiatrist is required to be on the ward and examine the patient.

To address some of these concerns about the psychodynamics of the staff as well as the patients, it is important to discuss a violent episode once it has occurred. This should be done among the staff as well as with the patient who was violent and among other patients on the ward. This is contrary to what staff usually wish to do. Once the episode is finished, they want to forget about it or deny it. The violent episode should be discussed in terms of what happened, what could have prevented it, why seclusion or restraint was used (if it was), and how the patient or the staff felt in terms of the use of seclusion or restraint. It is important that most patients will have negative reactions to being secluded and restrained. Among other patients on the ward, it is important to talk about the violent episode and why seclusion or restraint was used for that particular patient so as to allay other patients' fears that they could be secluded or restrained for no apparent reason in the future. A summary of the factors that decrease inappropriate seclusion or restraint is given in Table 1.

■ STANDARDS FOR SECLUSION AND RESTRAINT

In 1982 the Supreme Court heard the case of *Youngberg v Romeo* (2), the latter being a violent, profoundly mentally re-

TABLE 1. **Factors That Decrease Seclusion and Restraint**

- Adequate, trained staff
- Active treatment plans and opportunities for recreation
- Staff who listen and talk with patients
- Recognition of warning signs of violence escalation for the individual patient
- Knowing one's countertransference and other inappropriate reactions to a patient
- Knowing the ward dynamics and resolving conflicts between staff
- Discussion by staff after a violent episode has occurred
- Appropriate type and dose of medication

tarded man who was institutionalized. The Court ruled that he could be deprived of his liberty in terms of being restrained if it could be justified to protect others or himself, and if the decision was based on clinical judgment of a professional that is not a substantial departure from professional standards. The importance of this case is that the Court deferred to professional judgment rather than a rigid hierarchy of restrictiveness in the management of violence by patients. At the time the court decision was rendered, I was chairing a Task Force of the American Psychiatric Association (APA) to develop guidelines for the psychiatric uses of seclusion and restraint. The guidelines have been approved by the APA and have set reasonable minimal clinical standards for management of violence using seclusion and restraint in the context of verbal intervention, involuntary medication, and other factors in the treatment environment (3). The guidelines are expanded on in a book by members of the Task Force (4). These represent a minimal standard. More stringent guidelines at a local level would take precedence, such as for a state or individual hospital.

■ INDICATIONS FOR SECLUSION OR RESTRAINT

Indications for both seclusion and restraint are: 1) to prevent imminent harm to the patient or other persons when other means of control are not effective or appropriate; 2) to prevent serious disruption of the treatment program or significant damage to the physical environment; and 3) to assist in treatment as part of ongoing behavior therapy. Two additional indications pertain solely to seclusion: 4) to decrease the stimulation a patient receives, and 5) to comply with a patient's request. I will discuss the clinical aspects of these indications for seclusion and restraint.

One must consider the nature of the danger to the patient and to other persons, what constitutes "imminent" danger, and how one judges that other means of control are not effective or appropriate or that seclusion or restraint is a less restrictive mode of controlling dangerous behavior. The patient can be a danger to himself or herself in two ways: 1) in terms of deliberate suicidal acts or self-mutilation or 2) by a degree of excitement or behavioral dyscontrol that will result in exhaustion or injury if it continues. The patient can be a danger to others by deliberately trying to harm them through assault using a weapon or in other ways unintentionally endangering them as a result of marked disorganization of behavior.

Likewise, significant damage to the physical environment or the treatment milieu can be the result of deliberate behavior, as in antisocial or other personality disorders, or the result of grossly disorganized behavior, as in mania. Deliberate attempts to harm others or to damage the environment is often the result of psychotic thinking on a functional or organic basis. Most commonly this is manifested as paranoid delusional thoughts where the assault is seen by the patient as self-defense against others who are perceived as intending to harm the patient.

Disorganized and nondeliberate assault or other dangerous behavior may be the result of a number of clinical entities. This behavior is marked by impulsivity and often purposeless and uncontrolled activity. For these patients, hallucinations or delusions are often not related to the dangerous behavior. This may be found with nonparanoid schizophrenia, mania, or with organic brain synromes (e.g., phencyclidine-induced psychosis). Accompanying signs include loss of coherent speech, dysarthria, hyperactivity, fecal smearing and incontinence, screaming, or other manifestations.

If the etiology for the disorganized violent behavior is not known, restraint may be indicated so as to maintain the patient in the drug-free period for purposes of evaluation. Use of seclusion or restraint permits observation over time and differentiation of toxic from functional states. In addition, a violent patient may be preferentially managed in seclusion and restraint because of medical illness or drug allergies that would preclude the use of certain medications to control violent behavior.

Under certain circumstances, seclusion of a patient may be indicated for both the patient's benefit and that of the environment. Certain events, such as destruction of property, uncontrollable screaming or abuse, public masturbation, denudative behavior, uncontrolled intrusiveness on others, or fecal smearing, may constitute treatment indications for seclusion or restraint based on environmental needs. Clearly, however, this must be understood in conjunction with the patient's own needs.

Another issue for seclusion and restraint is whether these measures are to be used only once a patient is actually in the process of manifesting dangerous behavior as opposed to whether the staff may use these procedures in anticipation of imminent dangerous behavior by the patient. Once they are familiar with a particular patient, staff may rely on patterns of verbal or nonverbal phenomena that have occurred before violent episodes in the past. This is usually specific for the patient and may include such signs as escalating exited motor behavior, increase in muscle tone, pacing, and loud or profane speech, or more subtle manifestations such as the patient asking questions in a repetitive, persistent way. The use of specific previous patterns of behavior to justify seclusion or restraint must rely on a great degree of familiarity with the individual patient and must be documented.

Seclusion may be used for decreasing stimulation, usually for psychotic patients. The quiet atmosphere of the seclusion room is a relief from sensory overload, which may result even when a ward may appear quiet to other patients and staff.

Secluding a patient at the patient's own request represents a valid indication. The patient's wish to be in seclusion may be a responsible attempt to prevent sensory overload or to avert an incipient or escalating clinical state that would result in dangerous behavior. However, especially with patients with borderline personality, voluntary self-seclusion may serve regressive pathologic rather than therapeutic ends. Other often maladaptive requests for seclusion include those of the adolescent attempting to provoke staff, as well as the antisocial patient attempting to test the limits of staff tolerance or to foster a macho self-image. Thus the clinical differentiation of a meaning of a request for seclusion may require that some patients' requests for seclusion be refused and that alternative verbal or other interventions be offered. Other locales in the hospital such as the patient's room, courtyards, or a "music room" may be preferable for voluntary self-isolation. Indications for seclusion or restraint are summarized in Table 2.

■ ALTERNATIVES TO SECLUSION OR RESTRAINT

In using seclusion or restraint to prevent harm to the patient, other persons, or the environment, the staff must have considered or tried other means of control. Certainly verbal and other interventions such as socialization and recreation should be considered to prevent loss of control prior to resorting to seclusion or restraint. Patients must have continuing opportunities to participate in their environment, to become engaged in activities, and to talk and interact with staff and other patients. Recreational materials and structured activities should be readily available on all inpatient and day-hospital units where patients live or spend their time. Some patients need assistance and prompting to engage in recreational and rehabilitative activities productively. Thus a continuum of active outreach by staff is necessary to ensure that patients are engaged in an appropriate level of activity, given their deficits, assets, and symptomatic handicaps.

In terms of other alternatives, the use of medication as opposed to seclusion or restraint cannot be seen in the context of which option is less restrictive. The decision as to whether one

TABLE 2. **Indications for Seclusion or Restraint**

- To prevent imminent harm to others
- To prevent imminent harm to the patient
- To prevent serious disruption of the treatment environment

Specifically for Seclusion:

- To decrease stimulation a patient receives
- To comply with a patient's request

uses medication, seclusion, or restraint to control dangerous behavior must be made in terms of the individual patient. For example, the use of repetitive neuroleptic medication to control dangerous behavior in the developmentally disabled would not be as desirable as using restraint or seclusion first. On the other hand, involuntary medication may be preferred to seclusion and restraint in the case of a paranoid schizophrenic who is acting on paranoid delusions and has not been taking oral neuroleptic medication. With a patient in seclusion (e.g., a manic patient), less neuroleptic medication may be needed as stimulation is decreased.

■ CONTRAINDICATIONS FOR SECLUSION OR RESTRAINT

Seclusion or restraint may be contraindicated because of the patient's clinical or medical condition. The patient's unstable medical status, resulting from infection, cardiac illness, disorders of thermoregulation, or metabolic illness, may require close monitoring and close physical proximity of staff such that seclusion is not indicated. For certain such conditions, however, restraint may be valuable (e.g., in neurologic problems, such as delirium and dementia, where the patient's vulnerability to reduced sensory input may lead to worsening of the total clinical state, contraindicating seclusion).

Other situations representing relative contraindication to seclusion include those involving patients experiencing a paradoxical reaction to phenothiazine medications; patients who have just taken overdoses and require close monitoring; patients presenting with the symptoms of serious and uncontrollable self-abuse and self-mutilation; and the problem of seclusion rooms that cannot be sufficiently cooled on hot days for patients receiving drugs such as phenothiazines, which impair thermoregulation.

With physical restraint, an adverse effect is circulatory obstruction, which can be minimized by temporarily releasing one of four-point restraints every 15 minutes. Another adverse effect with restraints is aspiration. If a patient is lying on his or her back or is obstructed while restrained, one must guard against aspiration by constant monitoring.

Seclusion of a patient as a purely punitive response is

contraindicated. Similarly, a patient should never be secluded for the pure comfort or convenience of the staff, although it is common for patient and staff distress to coexist. While protection of other patients from harm is a valid indiction for seclusion, mere mild obnoxiousness, rudeness, or other unpleasantness to others is not. Finally, although staff anxiety is often a well-validated indicator, through contagion, of actual or incipient dangerousness in a patient, staff anxiety alone should not be a reason for secluding a patient. This distinction is not always easy to make on the clinical scene, but may be determined retrospectively by review with the staff. Contraindications for seclusion or restraint are summarized in Table 3.

■ ROLE OF THE PHYSICIAN

Beginning an episode of seclusion or restraint is usually an emergency procedure carried out by the nursing or other staff on an inpatient unit. However, except for behavior therapy, this requires a physician's review and order for continuation. Each institution has specific time parameters regarding review, and the psychiatrist should be familiar with them. The physician should be notified as soon as possible. The Task Force (3) preferred notification within one hour after the seclusion or restraint episode begins. For the first episode of seclusion or restraint, the physician should see the patient, usually within three hours and preferably within one hour after the beginning of the seclusion or restraint. When notified by telephone, the physician should indi-

TABLE 3. **Contraindications for Seclusion or Restraint**

- As punishment of the patient for some transgression
- For the pure comfort or convenience of the staff or other patients
- Unstable or unknown medical status with the patient in seclusion
- Delirium with the patient in seclusion
- Drug overdose with the patient in seclusion
- Self-mutilation with the patient in seclusion
- Patient on neuroleptics with a hot seclusion room that cannot be cooled
- Lack of constant monitoring for aspiration or circulatory obstruction with the patient in restraints

cate approval pending personal examination of the patient. During the visit, the physician should document this in the patient's record. This episode should be reviewed by the patient's physician and treatment team. For each subsequent seclusion or restraint episode for that patient, the physician should be notified within the hour. The Task Force believes that the physician, however, can exercise professional judgment as to whether an actual visit is indicated, and should indicate any special precautions that must be taken or monitoring that must be done by the nursing staff.

A physician should see the secluded or restrained patient as frequently as is necessary to monitor any changes in the patient's mental or physical status. Although the frequency of these visits may vary, a minimum of two visits a day (approximately 12 hours apart) is recommended. More frequent visits are necessary for certain patients, including those with concurrent medical problems, those receiving medical treatment that may complicate seclusion or restraint, those with organic brain syndrome, and those in situations where hyperthermia may occur and the patient needs to be closely monitored. When the physician sees the patient, the order for continued seclusion or restraint should be justified in terms of its continuation in the patient's record. During the visit, the physician should review the more frequent nursing observations of the patient in seclusion or restraint.

A physician's order for seclusion or restraint is generally valid for 12 hours. During the visit, a physician should examine the patient and document in the patient's record the reason for continued seclusion or restraint, taking into account the patient's mental and physical status, the degree of agitation, physical and emotional adverse effects of seclusion, and other factors such as staffing and the ability to handle the patient on the open inpatient unit. In some institutions, a large number of violent patients may mean that more than one patient will be in seclusion or restraint at a time. This strains the staff in terms of the need for observation, toileting, and other care of patients who are secluded and restrained. This may detract from unsecluded or unrestrained agitated patients. Thus, the condition of the ward, staffing, and types of patients must be considered in relation to whether a patient remains in seclusion or restraint.

Again it should be noted that guidelines for a specific hospital may be more restrictive than time parameters indicated in this book and that the clinician must adhere to hospital guidelines. The guidelines for seclusion and restraint within a specific hospital should be rehearsed and approved by the hospital staff as well as the legal staff. This includes specific techniques for putting a patient in seclusion, specific time parameters for physician's visits to the patient, and staff monitoring, as well as restraint devices such as four-point leather restraints or other devices.

■ TECHNIQUES OF SECLUSION AND RESTRAINT

The use of seclusion and restraint techniques places both staff and patients at risk for injury. This may be minimized by rehearsal of these techniques and adherence to the basic principles outlined in this book. Once the decision has been made to begin seclusion or restraint of an agitated patient, a seclusion or restraint leader is chosen from among the clinical staff. The leader should indicate the roles to be played by the remaining staff in the seclusion and restraint process. The leader should be chosen for familiarity with the patient or for other factors; for example, a female member of the staff may be more appropriate than a male member of the staff in terms of minimizing provocation and maximizing cooperation of the patient. Female staff members are usually considered less intimidating and less authoritarian than male staff members.

There should be adequate staff to control the patient's behavior if the patient refuses to comply with requests that he or she go into seclusion. This consists of at least five staff members, one for each extremity and one (who can be the seclusion leader) to control the patient's head. The staff should gather around the seclusion leader at the time of first contact with the violent patient. Staff should project an image of confidence and the ability to control the situation should the patient not cooperate. The area should be cleared of all other patients and physical obstructions leading to the seclusion room. Ideally there should be someone to observe the procedure, noting any injuries or difficulties with physical technique. This will make possible a critique of the seclusion or restraint procedure after the episode ends.

The onset of the seclusion or restraint procedure begins with telling the patient the reason for the procedure. The patient is given clear options in a nonthreatening or provocative way. For example, the patient may be told that his or her behavior is out of control and that he or she must go into seclusion so as to regain control. The patient is asked to walk quietly to the seclusion room accompanied by the staff. Having considered other forms of intervention, such as verbal ones or medication alone, further discussion or negotiation at this time is inappropriate. In fact, it may lead to an argument, physical fight, and injuries to the patient as well as staff. The patient is given a few seconds to comply; if the patient does not, the staff begins the seclusion or restraint procedure. At the time of the first contact with the patient and throughout the procedure, the staff must not humiliate or threaten the patient. They must maintain the patient's dignity and self-esteem.

Physical force begins after a prearranged signal from the seclusion leader. Each staff member grabs and controls one of the patient's extremities. Carefully so as not to injure the patient, the staff brings the patient to the ground through a backward motion, and each extremity is restrained at the joint by a member of the team. The patient's head should be controlled to prevent biting or neck injury. The staff should be cautious to avoid injuring the patient or causing pain. Not only is this inappropriate but it may interfere with future therapeutic relationships between the staff and the patient.

After the patient is restrained on the ground, additional staff may be called to assist in moving the patient to the seclusion room or to help apply physical restraints. The staff should lift the patient with the arms pressed into the sides and the legs held tightly at the knees. The head should be controlled and lifted as the back, hips, and legs are lifted.

Once the patient is in the seclusion room, the patient is put on his back with the head toward the seclusion door and feet in the opposite direction. Street clothes are removed, and special attention is paid to removing rings, belts, shoes, matches, and other potentially destructive objects. Medication may be injected at this time while the patient is physically restrained.

The staff exit in a coordinated manner, one at a time, releasing the legs first and then the arms last. The last staff member should move quickly in a backward fashion out of the seclusion room door, which is quickly locked. Another way of placing a patient in the seclusion room is to put the patient face down on a mattress with the head away from the door. Arms and legs may be brought behind the back, and it is possible for the last member of the team to control arms and legs while the patient is in this position. Again, the last staff member in the seclusion room should quickly release the arms and legs and leave the room. The latter technique may not be advisable for very obese patients because it may cause respiratory impairment in a facedown position.

After a patient has been placed in seclusion or restraint, the staff should discuss the episode among themselves so as to critique the technique as well as to allow verbalization of any conflicting feelings. The staff should also consider, especially on units where violence is rare, discussing the behavior that led up to the seclusion or restraint episode at community meetings with patients. Table 4 summarizes the process of secluding or restraining a patient.

■ MONITORING AND CARING FOR THE PATIENT

While the patient is in seclusion or restraint, there should be observations by the nursing staff at least every 15 minutes. These may be done by looking through the window of the seclusion room, especially for severely violent patients. In a written log, the staff should write their observations (e.g., "the patient is quiet," "the patient is walking around the seclusion room," or "the patient is yelling"). These visual checks are important so as to minimize patients harming themselves in the seclusion room. Of course, if self-mutilation is a concern, seclusion may not be indicated for the patient or constant observation of the patient in seclusion may be indicated.

A direct visit into the seclusion room is indicated at least every two hours. In the case of very violent patients, it is advisable that adequate number of staff accompany the nursing staff. During these visits, vital signs should be taken; meals, fluids, and toileting needs should be taken care of. All observations and recordings should be documented in the patient's record. In terms of care of the patient, the patient should be allowed to go to the

TABLE 4. **The Process of Secluding or Restraining a Patient**

- After verbal intervention or other means of controlling violent behavior have been considered or tried, a team of at least four staff and one leader should be formed.
- The staff should gather around the leader with an image of confidence and control of the situation.
- The leader should tell the patient he or she must go to the seclusion room or be put into restraints, briefly state the reason, and give directions.
- The patient is given a few seconds to comply, and further negotiation or discussion is not allowed.
- At a prearranged signal, each extremity is grabbed and controlled, and one staff member controls the patient's head.
- The patient is brought to the floor in a backward motion without being injured.
- Once on the floor, restraints are applied or the patient is carried to the seclusion room with uniform lifting of the body and control of extremities and the head.
- The patient is searched, and street clothes and dangerous objects such as rings, belts, shoes, and matches are removed.
- The patient is placed on his or her back with the head toward the door or face down with head away from the door.
- Staff exit one at a time in a coordinated manner.
- After the seclusion or restraint procedure is completed, staff should critique the process and discuss their feelings.
- During visits by staff, the patient should be assessed for degree of control of his or her behavior and for compliance with requests by the staff.
- The timing of gradual removal from seclusion or restraint is based on these assessments.
- Following removal from seclusion or restraint, staff should discuss with the patient his or her feelings about the procedure, what led up to the behavior, and what could have prevented it.

---

bathroom at least every four hours. In certain cases, this may mean taking the patient out of the seclusion room. Again, in the case of very violent patients, adequate staff should be present at that time. In the case of patients in restraints, the restraints will probably have to be removed while the patient is allowed to go to the bathroom.

Meals should be brought to the patient at regular intervals when the ward meals are served. Eating utensils, if any, should be blunt; even plastic knives and forks can be used as weapons. The patient should be instructed to sit at one corner of the seclusion room while the meal tray is placed in the seclusion room. If possible, the staff should be present with the patient while the meal is being eaten. This is to allow interpersonal contact with the patient as well as to make observations as to the degree of self-control. The reason for a patient eating alone should be documented in the patient's record. There should be adequate attention to fluid intake so as to prevent dehydration. Documentation of fluid intake is necessary in the patient's record.

The architecture and environment of the seclusion room should be free of hazards. Seclusion rooms are usually empty except for a mattress. The mattress should be constructed of durable foam and not fiber or other materials that the patient could use to hang or suffocate. The mattress should not be flammable and patients should be searched for matches prior to being placed in seclusion. The ceiling of the seclusion room should be high with recessed light fixtures. All walls and ceilings should be made of material that cannot be gouged out by patients. There should be no sharp edges to windows and no protuberances such as oxygen jets.

The staff should be able to observe every portion of the seclusion room; this may require reflectors. It is important that the staff be able to monitor patients so as to prevent self-mutilation and other injuries. If patients are very hyperactive and there is concern about exhaustion, then restraint with or without seclusion should be considered. If it appears that a patient's psychosis has become worse in the seclusion room, one should consider the impact of sensory deprivation in terms of this increase in psychosis. In this case, restraint may be indicated or constant attention by the staff may be indicated. Table 5 summarizes the process of assessing and monitoring the patient who is put into seclusion or restraint.

■ RELEASE FROM SECLUSION OR RESTRAINT

A patient may be released from seclusion or restraint when the patient's behavior is under control and no longer poses a

TABLE 5. **Assessing and Monitoring the Patient Who Is Put into Seclusion or Restraint**

- The physician should be notified and see the patient as soon after the seclusion or restraint as is possible for the first episode.
- For subsequent episodes, the physician should be notified and decide whether to see the patient.
- A physician should visit the patient in seclusion or restraint periodically.
- The reason for seclusion or restraint and the patient's medical as well as psychiatric status should be documented.
- Staff should observe the patient in seclusion or restraint at least every 15 minutes, and observations should be put into a written log.
- Staff should visit a patient in seclusion or restraint at least every two hours and take vital signs and care for the patient. This should be documented.
- Feeding, drinking, and toileting at appropriate intervals are necessary and should be documented.
- Patient should not be abandoned in seclusion or restraint.

danger to self or others or to further disruption of the treatment environment. The ability of a patient to control his or her behavior and to cooperate is evaluated throughout the seclusion episode. For example, during each visit, the patient's ability to respond to a verbal request should be judged. A patient may be asked to sit in a particular part of the seclusion room, or cooperation may be reflected in the patient becoming more amenable to taking oral medication rather than having to have injections. At a higher level, the patient will be able to cooperate with physical examinations, interviews, bathing, toileting, and other procedures.

Release from seclusion is a gradual process. The first step may be opening the seclusion room door for brief periods of time, followed by continued opening of the seclusion room door, to spending time alone in the patient's room, until the patient can be released to the general ward environment. Any evidence of loss of control or lack of cooperation should result in movement back to more restrictive steps in the procedure.

Following the episode of seclusion or restraint, the patient should be allowed to voice his or her feelings about the episode and should be questioned as to what led up to the behavior requiring seclusion or restraint as well as what could have been done to prevent the escalation.

Medication for the patient in seclusion and restraint is indicated in cases of severe agitation or psychotic psychopathology. Physicians should be cautioned, however, about overmedicating patients so that they become very lethargic, disorganized, and violent as a result of organic impairment. Injections of prn medication should not be used if the patient is in seclusion because this may result in varying doses of medication across nursing shifts, making assessment of the patient problematic. Instead, a fixed-dose regimen is preferable, with frequent evaluation by the physician. Use of medication in the emergency situation as well as in the long-term management of the violent patient are discussed in Chapters 5 and 7.

Some type of restraint device may be used so as to allow the patient to remain in the open ward setting. These devices include bindings of the wrist to a belt around the patient's waist, or binding patients to a wheelchair so that they can participate in group meetings and other activities of the ward. Attention should be given, however, to the protection of these patients so that they are not injured by other patients on the inpatient unit.

■ REFERENCES

1. Lion JR, Pasternak SA: Countertransference reactions to violent patients. Am J Psychiatry 1973; 130:207–210
2. *Youngberg v Romeo,* 102 Supreme Ct 2452 (1982)
3. Tardiff K: Seclusion and Restraint: The Psychiatric Uses: Task Force Report No. 22. Washington, DC, American Psychiatric Association, 1985
4. Tardiff K (ed): The Psychiatric Uses of Seclusion and Restraint. Washington, DC, American Psychiatric Press, 1984

USE OF 5
EMERGENCY MEDICATION

Emergency medication is useful for psychotic violent patients; it is often used in conjunction with seclusion or restraint. Emergency medication is indicated for nonpsychotic, violent patients when verbal intervention is not appropriate or effective. It may be used instead of seclusion or restraint. On the other hand, it may be used with seclusion or restraint when severe agitation or violence is present to minimize detrimental effects violence may have on patients even though they are secluded or restrained. Table 1 lists the doses of medication recommended in emergencies for violent patients.

■ NEUROLEPTICS

I believe that neuroleptic medication should be used primarily for the management of violent patients who manifest psychotic symptomatology. Occasionally it may be indicated for patients who are not psychotic but who are violent, as in the case of patients with organic brain dysfunction where anxiolytic agents or sedatives may exacerbate the clinical picture. In the emergency situation, neuroleptic medication is often given im due to circumstances, namely that the psychotic patient is completely out of control. It may be offered by mouth, with the clear stipulation that if the patient does not take the medication, the medication will be given im to manage violence that is a danger to others or to the patient. The use of neuroleptic medication in the nonemergency situation where the patient takes medication by mouth is discussed in Chapter 7.

Soloff (1) reviewed the literature on the use of rapid neuroleptization and the acute management of the violent patient. He indicated that a wide range of drugs can be used in this procedure and that there is general safety and efficacy with rapid neuroleptization. It has been demonstrated effective with schizophrenic and manic patients in terms of improvement of delusions, hallucinations, disorganized thought, and agitation and violence. There are two basic strategies in this approach: the use of high-

TABLE 1. **Doses of Medication Recommended in Emergencies for Violent Patients**

1. **Rapid Neuroleptization**[a]
   A. High Potency
      Low-dose haloperidol 5 mg (1 ml) im every four to eight hours
         Maximum daily dose 15 to 30 mg
      High-dose haloperidol 10 mg (2 ml) im every 30 minutes
         Maximum daily dose 45 to 100 mg
   B. Low Potency
      A test dose of chlorpromazine 10 to 25 mg im is given, and the
      patient is observed for postural hypotension. If not a problem:
      Low-dose: chlorpromazine 25 mg (1 ml) im every four hours
         Maximum daily dose 150 mg
      High-dose: chlorpromazine 75 mg (3 ml) im every four hours
         Maximum daily dose 400 mg; not more than 3 ml should be
         injected at each site

2. **Benzodiazepines (with or without neuroleptics)**
   Lorazepam 2 to 4 mg by mouth every four to six hours
      Maximum daily dose 10 mg
   Lorazepam 2 to 4 mg (1 to 2 ml) im every one to two hours
      Maximum daily dose 10 mg
   Lorazepam[b] 2 to 4 mg (1 to 2 ml) iv slowly at the rate of 2 mg
   (1 ml) per minute repeated at 10-minute intervals
      Maximum daily dose 10 mg

3. **Barbiturates**
   Sodium amobarbital[b] 200 to 500 mg (10 percent aqueous solution)
   IV slowly so as not to exceed 1 ml/minute. Dose is determined
   largely by the patient's response.

Note. Doses should be adjusted based on the patient's age, weight, debilitation, and other clinical considerations.

[a]Neuroleptics other than haloperidol and chlorpromazine may be used in doses relative to the ones recommended here.

[b]These drugs should be used intravenously only for active, severe violence or agitation, with resuscitation equipment and trained staff nearby.

potency neuroleptic drugs with an anxiolytic or other drug for sedation if necessary versus low-potency neuroleptic drugs for their sedative side effects as well as antipsychotic effects.

Although I favor the use of high-potency neuroleptic drugs with or without concurrent lorazepam, the choice of strategy should also take into consideration the patient's history and physical status. One should attempt to review the patient's previous responses to medication as well as the presence of medical illnesses that may predispose to or be exacerbated by extrapyramidal side effects or orthostatic hypotension. If extrapyramidal side effects are less acceptable, low-potency neuroleptics should be used; if orthostatic hypotension and related side effects are less acceptable, then high-potency neuroleptics are indicated. The physician, of course, should be free to change strategy as the patient's medical condition is monitored.

The use of high-potency drugs with rapid neuroleptization often employs haloperidol. There are two approaches with the high-potency neuroleptic strategy. The first is a low-dose approach using haloperidol 5 mg (1 ml) im every four to eight hours for a maximum dose of 15 to 30 mg/day. The high-dose approach uses haloperidol 10 mg (2 ml) im every 30 minutes with a 24-hour maximum dose of 45 to 100 mg. Most patients treated for violence and acute psychosis will usually need 15 to 60 mg/day. Improvement in terms of decreased violence and hostility is rapid, often within 20 minutes of the initial injection of haloperidol when given 10 mg im.

With rapid neuroleptization, one should be cautious to exclude patients who are delirious or otherwise organically impaired because the sedative or anticholinergic effects of the neuroleptics may exacerbate such conditions. Likewise, intoxication with alcohol or other sedative drugs is a contraindication to rapid neuroleptization because the patient's level of consciousness may be impaired. Use of these medications in alcohol withdrawal is also contraindicated because they decrease the seizure threshold. Extrapyramidal symptoms such as akathesia may produce a paradoxical reaction, with increase of agitation and violence. Other serious side effects include neuroleptic malignant syndrome, which is described in Chapter 7, and (very rarely) laryngeal dystonic reaction.

Low-potency neuroleptic medications are used less frequently than the high-potency neuroleptic medications because of problems with orthostatic hypotension and because the sedation obtained by the use of low-potency neuroleptics can also be obtained through the use of lorazepam with high-potency neuroleptic medication. If the low-potency neuroleptic strategy is to be used, chlorpromazine is usually the drug of choice. A test dose of chlorpromazine 10 to 25 mg im is recommended, and the patient is observed for orthostatic hypotension. If this is not a problem, chlorpromazine should be given 25 mg im (1 ml) every four hours in a low-dose approach or up to 75 mg (3 ml) every four hours for the high-dose approach. The maximum daily dose for chlorpromazine im is 400 mg. No more than 3 ml should be injected at each injection because local tissue irritation may result. Vital signs should be monitored. If there is an extreme hypotensive crisis (i.e., the systolic blood pressure is less than 80 mm Hg on rising), the patient will require treatment with vasopressors such as metaraminol bitartrate or levarterenol bitartrate. Epinephrine is contraindicated because it may further lower blood pressure in neuroleptic-induced orthostatic hypotension.

Using either approach, once the patient's violence is under control oral medication may be started using a milligram-for-milligram translation on a 24-hour basis and allowing for further im prn doses in case of recurrences of violent behavior. Other clinicians suggest oral doses one-and-a-half times the im dose administered in the first 24 hours. Oral medication should be given in liquid form and divided into two or more doses, depending on the clinical situation. Other side effects of the neuroleptic medication are discussed in Chapter 7.

■ ANXIOLYTICS

The benzodiazepines can be used very effectively in emergency situations where violence is in the process of occurring or where it is imminent. Benzodiazepines may be used with the neuroleptic medications for schizophrenics, manics, and patients in other psychotic states, or they may be used alone for the management of nonpsychotic patients. For patients who appear to have some degree of control, they may be offered as oral medication. However, in most emergency situations, benzodiazepines are used im or iv. A number of clinicians are cautious about their use because there have been reports of paradoxical violence. Aggressive dyscontrol in patients treated with benzodiazepines appears to be overstated and is not frequent, with the possible exceptions of clonazepam and alprazolam (2).

The safest and most rapid method of administering the benzodiazepines is by im injection rather than iv. In view of this, I prefer lorazepam because it is reliably and rapidly absorbed from injection sites, unlike diazepam or chlordiazepoxide. Lorazepam also is useful because it produces sedation for a longer period of time than diazepam because it remains in the circulation rather than being absorbed into tissues. On the other hand, the half-life of lorazepam is 12 hours, much shorter than diazepam, so that accumulation is not as problematic as it is with diazepam. Lorazepam, given by im injection, rapidly begins to enter the circulation and produces sedation within an hour. The oral administration of lorazepam produces more gradual effects, with sedation occurring usually longer than one hour and less than four hours after administration.

I recommend 2 to 4 mg by mouth or im. A subsequent 2- to 4-mg dose can be repeated if there is continued agitation and aggression at a time depending on the route of administration (i.e., in an hour or so if im or four to six hours if by mouth). Often this is sufficient to manage violence in the emergency situation. After the emergency has subsided, lower maintenance levels of lorazepam with or without neuroleptics to a maximum of 10 mg/ day in three divided doses can be given. Lorazepam up to 4 mg for an average-size person could be given iv, but given slowly at the rate of 2 mg (1 ml) per minute so as to avoid respiratory depression. This can be repeated in 10 minutes if needed (3). This route of administration should be used only in severe violence. Resuscitation equipment and staff able to use this equipment should be nearby; laryngospasm or respiratory depression are potential side effects.

■ BARBITURATES

The barbiturate usually used to induce sedation or sleep in violent patients in the emergency situation is sodium amobarbital, administered intravenously in 10 percent aqueous solution. The total dose used is from 200 to 500 mg; the rate of administration should not exceed 1 ml/minute (3). While administering the medication, one should attempt to achieve sedation or sleep without depressing respiration. Because respiratory depression and laryngospasm are possible side effects, resuscitation equipment must be nearby. The beneficial effect of this medication occurs within a few minutes. The dose may be repeated if the patient becomes more agitated and aggressive later. I stress that this should be used only in extreme emergencies and usually requires concurrent restraint of the patient while administration of sodium amobarbital is taking place. My preference is to use lorazepam with restraint until the medication takes effect instead of sodium amobarbital iv.

■ REFERENCES

1. Soloff PH: Emergency management of the violent patient, in The American Psychiatric Association Annual Review, vol 6. Edited by Hales RE, Frances AJ. Washington, DC, American Psychiatric Press, 1987
2. Dietch JT, Jennings RK: Aggressive dyscontrol in patients treated with benzodiazepines. J Clin Psychiatry 1988; 49:184–188
3. American Medical Association: AMA Drug Evaluations. Chicago, American Medical Association, 1986

6 EXTENDED EVALUATION OF VIOLENT PATIENTS

Once the emergency situation is under control, the clinician may take more time to evaluate the patient to determine the etiology of the violent behavior and to plan treatment. Issues such as safety of the clinician and others as well as the physical environment of the office or other setting in which the violent patient is interviewed have been discussed earlier and pertain here as well. The same elements of the verbal techniques described in Chapter 3 to intervene in the emergency situation are relevant in the interview of the violent patient for purposes of gathering history. One speaks to the patient in a calm, nonprovocative, nonjudgmental manner. The clinician should not intimidate the patient in any way and should show respect for the patient. It is important that the patient get a sense that the clinician is in control of the situation, but not in an authoritarian manner. The primary goal of the early phase of the interview is to facilitate the patient talking because often violent patients have difficulty expressing their concerns verbally.

In making an assessment of the violent patient, the clinician should also turn to other sources of information, such as past medical records, the police (who may have brought the patient to the hospital), relatives, the patient's therapist, and the medical physician. I prefer to interview the violent patient before going to these other sources of information. If the police bring the patient to the hospital, however, they may have to be interviewed before they leave. One should ask them to stay, but this is not always possible.

■ CHIEF COMPLAINT

The clinician should record the patient's stated reasons for being in the evaluation or treatment setting at that point in time. The clinician should evaluate the complaint as stated by the patient, even though the patient's stated chief complaint may not agree with other sources of information—for example, the police stating that an adolescent boy tried to kill his mother with a kitchen knife because he said that she was the devil. In this case, the young man may say that he came for an evaluation because he was having difficulties in school and with his parents. Although the clinician would fully evaluate the violence later, it is important in the early phase of evaluation to let the patient present his or her view of the problems 1) to assess the patient's perspective of what the problem is, 2) to assess the patient's accuracy and reliability, and 3) to avoid confrontation in the early phase, which would impede subsequent evaluation.

■ HISTORY OF THE PRESENTING ILLNESS

Although all aspects of the patient's present psychiatric illness should be assessed in the interview, I will focus on the history of violence associated with psychiatric illness. There should be the determination of the onset of the first violent episode and the development of a chronology of violence since then. Questions should be asked about the frequency and target of violent behavior, with particular efforts to identify recurring patterns of escalation and violence (e.g., a husband arriving home after work after a few drinks, being very demanding, with the wife countering by pointing out his deficiencies, followed by escalation of hostility and eventual violence). There should be the determination of the severity in terms of degree of injury or intended injury. Any associated symptoms either preceding or during the violent episode (e.g., amnesia) should be explored. The clinician should inquire as to prior evaluations of the violent behavior, including tests done, such as an electroencephalogram (EEG) and diagnostic imaging. Likewise, a detailed history of treatment, including medication and hospitalizations related to violence and other disorders, should be documented. Records of evaluations and treatments should be requested from these institutions.

The clinician should inquire about other types of violence, particularly that of an impulsive nature. This includes any criminal offenses, past suicidal ideation and behavior, and behavior such as reckless driving, destruction of property, fire setting, reckless spending, and sexual acting-out.

■ FAMILY HISTORY

In addition to the routine family history consisting of the names of relatives, ages of those living, causes of death for those deceased, and any psychiatric illnesses, the clinician should focus on situations that can lead to violence. Adolescents and other violent individuals often come from chaotic family situations. There is parental psychopathology associated with marital discord, broken homes, and inability to supervise and discipline children adequately. It is important to understand familial and cultural values and norms concerning the expression of violence. Often this is related to low socioeconomic status and poverty, not racial characteristics. Of utmost importance is the occurrence of violence within the family unit: spouse abuse, child abuse, or other types of violence between family members. Whether this may point to a genetic predisposition or a child modeling parents and other family members is unclear. What is clear is that a history of being physically abused or observing physical abuse within the family unit is related to subsequent violence as an adult (1).

■ PERSONAL AND DEVELOPMENTAL HISTORY

Information about perinatal complications should be elicited as well as subsequent accidents and injuries, particularly involving loss of consciousness, dizziness, or headaches. As stated earlier, there should be assessment of history of abuse as a child or a history of other domestic violence as the patient was growing up. Difficulties in terms of reading and other learning disabilities should be considered in light of the patient's educational attainment. There should be a description of the relationships between the patient and peers as well as family members.

■ MEDICAL HISTORY

As will be discussed later in this chapter, a wide range of medical illnesses have been found to be associated with violent behavior. Any medical illnesses and any past or current medication should be documented in the record. Of great importance is assessment of history and current state of alcohol and substance abuse. A summary of information that should be sought about the history of violence is given in Table 1.

TABLE 1. **Information About the History of Violence**

- Date of onset
- Frequency and target(s) of violent behavior
- Recurring patterns and escalation
- Severity of injuries to others
- Symptoms associated with violent episodes
- History of previous diagnostic testing and imaging and where they were done (to obtain records)
- History of other impulsive behavior such as suicidal behavior, destruction of property, reckless driving, reckless spending, sexual acting-out, fire setting, and criminal offenses
- History of familial violence as a child (e.g., being abused as a child, other intrafamilial violence)
- History of head injury, birth complications, serious childhood diseases, and other developmental problems
- Past and current medical illnesses (see Tables 3 and 4)

■ MENTAL STATUS AND PHYSICAL EXAMINATIONS

Rather than organize psychopathology and physical findings in the usual structure of the mental status and physical examinations, I will organize psychopathology and physical findings around diagnostic groups found to be associated with violence.

ORGANIC DISORDERS

As a result of impaired thinking and perceptual disturbances, violence in organic mental disorders and syndromes may be the result of decreased control over aggressive and other impulses with poor social judgment as well as the result of paranoid thoughts or even delusions in these patients who feel threatened by their cognitive impairment. In delirium, there may be increased psychomotor activity with violence accompanied by disordered thinking, fluctuating level of consciousness, perceptual disturbances, disorientation, and memory impairment. In dementia, patients are more alert but can be irritable, hostile, and violent as a result of their frustration with impaired memory and higher cortical function. In addition, suspicious, irritable personalities may be intensified with dementia.

In organic delusional syndrome, there are prominent delusions that may lead to retaliation and violence against others if of a paranoid nature. In organic hallucinosis, a prominent symptom is that of hallucinations that may lead to violence against others if threatening or derogatory. In organic mood syndrome, a manic state with hyperactivity and disorganization may lead to violence toward others.

In organic personality syndrome, by definition, there are recurrent outbreaks of aggression out of proportion to any precipitating factors as well as unstable mood and impaired social judgment with impulsivity. In addition, these patients may be suspicious or paranoid and, as a result, violent.

Intoxication is a residual category of organic mental disorder for cases that do not fit into any of the above categories and that result from recent psychoactive substance use. Alcohol and a number of substances can produce belligerence and violence through a number of mechanisms such as disinhibition, stimula-

Progress in Psychiatry

The Continuation Order Plan is available for institutions only. (Individuals are encouraged to enroll through their institutions.)

Please rush enrollment information to the following:

Name

Institution

Address

City _____ State _____ Zip _____

Telephone ( )

Mail to:

American Psychiatric Press, Inc.
Continuation Orders Department
1400 K Street, N.W., Suite 1101, Washington, DC 20005

American Psychiatric Press, Inc.

■ **Concise Guide to Consultation Psychiatry**
Michael G. Wise, MD and James R. Rundell, MD
Order #8123 $16.95 Paperback

■ **Concise Guide to Group Psychotherapy**
Sophia Vinogradov, MD and Irvin D. Yalom, MD
Order #8327 $16.95 Paperback

■ **Concise Guide to Laboratory and Diagnostic Testing in Psychiatry**
Richard B. Rosse, MD, Alexis A. Geise, MD,
Stephen I. Deutsch, MD, PhD, and John M. Morihisa, MD
Order #8333 $17.95 Paperback

■ **Concise Guide to Somatic Therapies in Psychiatry**
Laurence B. Guttmacher, MD
Order #8122 $17.95

■ **Concise Guide to Treatment of Alcoholism and Addictions**
Richard J. Frances, MD and John E. Franklin, MD
Order #8326 $16.95

Concise Guides

Series Editor: Robert E. Hales, MD

The Concise Guides provide, in a most accessible format, practical information for psychiatrists—and especially for psychiatry residents and medical students—working in such varied treatment settings as inpatient psychiatry services, outpatient clinics, consultation-liaison services, and private practice. These guides are meant to complement the more detailed information to be found in lengthier psychiatry texts. The books in this series contain a detailed Table of Contents, along with an index, tables and charts, for easy access; and their size, designed to fit into a lab coat pocket, makes them a convenient source of up-to-date information.

■ **Concise Guide to Assessment and Management of Violent Patients**
Kenneth Tardiff, MD, MPH
Order #8142 $16.95 Paperback

■ **Concise Guide to Clinical Psychiatry**
Stephen L. Dubovsky, MD
Order #8331 $17.95 Paperback

■ **Concise Guide to Clinical Psychiatry and the Law**

tion, or delusional thinking. Withdrawal is a residual category for organic mental disorders that do not fit into any of the above categories and that result from cessation or reduction of psychoactive substance use.

PSYCHOACTIVE SUBSTANCES

ALCOHOL

The ingestion of alcohol often may be associated with aggression and violence as a result of disinhibition, particularly in the initial phase of intoxication. Intoxication is accompanied by emotional lability and impaired judgment. The patient may appear to have slurred speech, incoordination, unsteady gait, nystagmus, and a flushed face. Violent behavior can also be found in persons who drink small amounts of alcohol insufficient to cause intoxication in most people. This is known as the alcohol idiosyncratic intoxication.

Violence may be associated with alcohol withdrawal after cessation of prolonged, heavy ingestion of alcohol for two or three days. This is manifested by coarse tremor of the hands, tongue, or eyelids and at least one of the following: nausea or vomiting, weakness, autonomic hyperactivity, anxiety, depressed mood or irritability, hallucinations (which may be transient or more persistent), headache, or insomnia. In some cases, alcohol withdrawal may be manifested by delirium. Violence may result from gross disorganization of behavior or in response to threatening auditory hallucinations.

SEDATIVES OR ANXIOLYTICS

Although sedative or anxiolytic substances can produce violence with intoxication, this is less frequent than with alcohol intoxication. The mechanism of action, however, appears to be the same, namely that of disinhibition and, as a result, acting-out of aggressive or sexual impulses, with mood lability and impaired judgment. The patient may have slurred speech, incoordination, unsteady gait, or impairment in attention or memory.

As with alcohol, withdrawal from sedatives or anxiolytic substances may be associated with violence and irritability following cessation of prolonged (several weeks or more) moderate or heavy use of these substances. In addition, at least three of the following are found: nausea or vomiting; weakness; autonomic hyperactivity; orthostatic hypotension; coarse tremor of the hands, tongue, and eyelids; insomnia; and, in some cases, grand mal seizures. In certain cases, delirium may be present with vivid threatening hallucinations and delusional thinking, with resulting violence.

COCAINE OR CRACK

Cocaine, particularly through the nasal route, initially produces a feeling of well-being and euphoria. With continued use, particularly intravenously or smoked in the form of crack, euphoria turns to grandiosity, psychomotor agitation, suspiciousness, and, frequently, violence. With continued use, suspiciousness becomes paranoid ideation and, subsequently, paranoid delusional thinking. Thus violence results from delusional thinking as well as the effect of cocaine through overall stimulation. A person using cocaine has pupilary dilatation, chills, nausea or vomiting, tachycardia, and elevated blood pressure and may be perspiring and have hallucinations, particularly visual or tactile in nature. Unlike alcohol and the sedative-anxiolytic substances, cocaine withdrawal is not usually associated with violence but rather with depression. In some cases of prolonged use, cessation of cocaine use can result in profound impairment in thinking, suicidal behavior, irritability, and psychomotor agitation. Irritability, agitation, and, in some cases, paranoid ideation may result in violence. Intense craving for more cocaine when supplies have been exhausted may also lead to violence while the addict obtains cocaine or money for its purchase.

AMPHETAMINES OR OTHER SYMPATHOMIMETICS

With intense or prolonged amphetamine use, a feeling of well-being and confidence turns to confusion, rambling, incoherence, paranoid ideation, and delusional thinking. With this there are agitation, fighting, and other forms of aggression and impaired social judgment. The patient appears to have pupilary dilatation, may be perspiring, or may have chills, nausea and vomiting, tachycardia, and elevated blood pressure.

Amphetamine withdrawal, like cocaine withdrawal, is usually manifested by depression and insomnia, although there may be psychomotor agitation and paranoid ideation following prolonged heavy use of amphetamines or similar substances. The symptoms may persist more than 24 hours after cessation of use of amphetamines.

HALLUCINOGENS

Hallucinogens such as D-lysergic acid diethylamide (LSD), dimethyltryptamine (DMT), and mescaline may result in impaired judgment and paranoid ideation in addition to other perceptual changes, including depersonalization, derealization, illusions, synesthesias, and hallucinations. Hallucinations are usually visual. The person may have marked anxiety and a fear of losing his or her mind; will appear with pupilary dilatation, sweating, tremors, and incoordination; and may have tachycardia, palpitations, and blurring of vision.

Violence may occur during intoxication with the above-mentioned hallucinogens, but it is not as common as in phencyclidine (PCP) intoxication. Within one hour of oral use (five minutes if smoked or taken intravenously), PCP often produces marked violence, impulsivity, unpredictability, and grossly impaired judgment. There may be delusional thinking or delirium. The patient may have vertical or horizontal nystagmus; be ataxic and dysarthric; and manifest increased blood pressure or heart rate, numbness or diminished responsiveness to pain, muscle rigidity, and hyperacusis. The patient may manifest seizures. There may be persistent psychopathology following PCP use; with other hallucinogens, except for occasional flashbacks, there is little residual psychopathology after limited use. Flashbacks are more often a source of great anxiety for the patient rather than associated with violent behavior.

INHALANTS

Inhalants are hydrocarbons found in substances such as gasoline, glue, paint, and paint thinners. These are often used by young children and early adolescents to produce intoxication, which may be characterized by belligerence and violence as well as impaired judgment. Chronic or heavy use of inhalants may produce neurologic signs such as incoordination, general muscle weakness, and psychomotor retardation. The patient may manifest, even with mild use, dizziness, nystagmus, incoordination, slurred speech, unsteady gait, lethargy, depressed reflexes, psychomotor retardation, tremor, general muscle weakness, blurred vision, stupor, or euphoria.

OTHER SUBSTANCES

Prescription drugs may cause violence either by excessive doses or through side effects. Examples of this are anticholinergic medications, which can produce violence, and steroids. In addition, akathisia from neuroleptic medications may be interpreted as intended violence or aggression. A list of substances related to violent behavior in the intoxicated state or in withdrawal is given in Table 2.

PRIMARY DISEASES OF THE BRAIN ASSOCIATED WITH VIOLENCE

A number of primary diseases of the brain can be associated with violent behavior. Violence in temporal lobe epilepsy is not frequent. When it occurs, it may occur during the ictal period; if so, it is often purposeless. Violence has also been found in the interictal period among patients with temporal lobe epilepsy. In the postictal period following generalized seizures, violence has been found with encephalopathy. Infections of the brain, including viral encephalitis, acquired immune deficiency syndrome (AIDS), tuberculosis and fungal meningitis, syphilis, and herpes simplex can be associated with violent behavior.

Other primary diseases of the brain associated with violence include head trauma, normal pressure hydrocephalus, cerebrovascular diseases, tumors, Huntington's chorea, multiple sclero-

---

TABLE 2. **Substance Use and Abuse Related to Violence**

Alcohol: intoxication and withdrawal
Sedatives and anxiolytics: intoxication and withdrawal
Cocaine: intoxication and withdrawal
Amphetamines: intoxication
Hallucinogens: intoxication (especially phencyclidine)
Inhalants: intoxication (e.g., glue, gasoline)
Other prescription drugs: intoxication (e.g., anticholinergic drugs, steroids)

sis, Alzheimer's disease, Pick's disease, multi-infarct dementia, Parkinson's disease, Wilson's disease, and postanoxic or posthypoglycemic states with brain damage. Primary diseases of the brain associated with violence are listed in Table 3.

SYSTEMIC DISORDERS ASSOCIATED WITH VIOLENCE

There are a number of systemic disorders associated with violence. Unlike the primary diseases of the brain, many of these are treatable and reversible. Thus, recognition is important, and appropriate medical care is necessary. These disorders include hypoxia; electrolyte imbalances; hepatic disease; renal disease; vitamin deficiencies such as B_{12} folate or thiamine; systemic infections; hypoglycemia; Cushing's disease; hyperthyroidism; hypothyroidism; systemic lupus erythematosus; poisoning by heavy metals, insecticides, and other substances; and porphyria. Systemic disorders associated with violence are listed in Table 4.

TABLE 3. **Primary Diseases of the Brain Associated with Violence**

- Temporal lobe epilepsy (partial complex seizures)
- General seizure postictal encephalopathy
- Head trauma
- Infections (including viral encephalitis, acquired immune deficiency syndrome (AIDS), tuberculosis and fungal meningitis, syphilis, herpes simplex)
- Normal pressure hydrocephalus
- Cerebrovascular diseases
- Tumors
- Huntington's chorea
- Multiple sclerosis
- Alzheimer's disease
- Pick's disease
- Multi-infarcts
- Parkinson's disease
- Wilson's disease
- Postanoxic or posthypoglycemic states

TABLE 4. **Systemic Disorders Associated with Violence**

- Hypoxia
- Electrolyte imbalances
- Hepatic disease
- Renal disease
- Vitamin deficiencies (B-12 folate, thiamine)
- Systemic infections
- Hypoglycemia
- Cushing's disease
- Hyper- or hypothyroidism
- Systemic lupus erythematosus
- Heavy metals, insecticides, and other poisons
- Porphyria

SCHIZOPHRENIA

Having excluded a gross organic cause for violent behavior, the next group of violent patients to be discussed are schizophrenics. In paranoid schizophrenia, there is delusional thinking in terms of persecution. Patients may believe that people are trying to harm them, that the police or FBI is spying on them, that some unknown mechanism is controlling their minds, or that the therapist is harming them (e.g., through medication). Paranoid schizophrenics may react to these persecutory delusions by retaliating against the presumed source of this persecution. Other types of schizophrenics may attempt to kill others because of some form of psychotic identification with the victim, usually a well-known entertainer, a political figure, or (in some cases) the patient's therapist. Hallucinations associated with schizophrenia, particularly command hallucinations (e.g., the patient is commanded by God to kill someone), have been known to result in violent behavior and homicide. In addition, hallucinations in which people are cursing or insulting the patient may result in retaliation against a supposed source of these insults.

Sudden unpredictable changes in affect may be associated with anger, aggression, and violent behavior. Some schizophrenics are violent because of generalized disorganization of thought and a lack of impulse control, with purposeless, excited psychomotor activity resulting in violence. A key diagnostic point to remember is that schizophrenics have intact orientation and memory; violent patients with organic mental disorders do not.

DELUSIONAL (PARANOID) DISORDER

Although delusional disorder is uncommon, it can often be associated with violence. The persistent nonbizarre delusion possessed by these patients may be of the persecutory type in which patients feel conspired against, cheated, spied on, poisoned, or otherwise harmed. In addition to resorting to legal action and appeal to government agencies, patients with this disorder often become resentful and angry and may become violent against those they believe are harming them. Delusional disorders of the jealous type involve the persistent belief that the patient's spouse or lover is unfaithful. These patients attempt to restrict the activities of and follow the spouse or lover. They may resort to physical attacks on the spouse or lover or someone who is identified as the "other partner" in this "infidelity."

MOOD DISORDERS

Manic patients may be violent as a result of their extreme psychomotor agitation or as a result of irritable mood associated with angry tirades. Most violence by manic patients is not premeditated and is purposeless. Rarely, a manic patient may become violent as a result of delusional thinking where the patient believes he or she is being persecuted because of some special attribute. It is usually the case with the manic that all impulses are put into action. If some of these impulses are violent, then they too become violent actions.

Other patients with mood disorders are rarely violent. An infrequent exception is the psychotic depressed patient. In this type of patient, extreme hopelessness, feelings that life is not worth living, or delusional feelings of profound guilt may result in violence, usually involving murder, followed by suicide. If this occurs, it most often involves a woman killing her children and then herself, or a man killing his family and then himself. Obviously, the clinician is not called on to evaluate such a patient unless the suicide attempt has failed.

PERSONALITY DISORDERS

The intermittent explosive personality disorder in DSM-III-R (2) is subsumed under the diagnosis of organic personality syndrome, which has been discussed earlier in this chapter. A key characteristic of this syndrome is the episodic recurrent outburst of aggression and violence that is grossly out of proportion to any precipitating psychosocial stressor. There is often remorse following this violent episode (e.g., the case of a husband who has attacked his wife or a mother who has severely beaten a child). There is little evidence of other behavioral problems between these violent episodes.

This is in distinction to two other personality disorders associated with violence: the borderline personality and the antisocial personality. In the case of the borderline personality disorder, in addition to exhibiting frequent displays of anger and recurrent physical violence toward others, the borderline personality patient manifests other behavioral problems between the violent episodes. There is often a wide range of impulsive behaviors, including suicidal or self-mutilating behaviors, excessive spending, indiscreet sexual behavior, drug abuse, shoplifting, and reckless driving. In addition, there is a marked and persistent identity problem manifested by uncertainty about self-image, sexual orientation, career goals, and other values. There are often manipulative attempts to obtain caring from others.

Violence manifested by persons with the antisocial personality disorder is just one of many antisocial behaviors. These patients repeatedly get into physical fights and violence involving their spouses, children, and individuals outside of the family. A number of other antisocial behaviors include destroying property, harassing others, stealing, engaging in illegal occupations, driving in a reckless or intoxicated manner, and being involved in promiscuous relationships. The patient often lies, does not honor financial obligations, and is unable to sustain consistent employment. Alcohol and substance abuse are often a problem. The violence toward others and other aspects of antisocial behavior are not accompanied by remorse or guilt.

MENTAL RETARDATION

Although most patients with mental retardation are not violent, when violence does occur it is often difficult to treat. Violence due to poor intellectual ability is associated with anger and frustration at not being able to obtain what is desired or at not being able to verbalize concerns and feelings. This is accompanied by poor impulse control and then violence toward others or the self. Some of the causes of mental retardation can be subsumed under organic mental disorders (e.g., head trauma during birth or as an adult, hypoxia and lead poisoning in childhood).

DISRUPTIVE BEHAVIOR DISORDERS

These disorders occur in children and adolescents. However, they may continue into adulthood—conduct disorder becoming antisocial personality and attention-deficit hyperactivity disorder persisting in terms of aggressive violent behavior. Children or adolescents with conduct disorders are often aggressive. There may be physical violence toward others and cruelty to others or to animals. They may deliberately destroy property (e.g., fire setting). They also engage in stealing, mugging, purse snatching, robbery, and (later in adolescence) rape. Often there is abuse of alcohol and other substances and early sexual behavior in childhood. Violence and other antisocial disruptive behaviors are not accompanied by remorse or guilt. There is low frustration tolerance and low self-esteem. Adolescents with this disorder may manifest violence and other conduct problems, either as part of a group activity with peers or in an isolated solitary manner not part of a group activity.

Children and adolescents with attention-deficit hyperactivity disorder are less frequently maliciously violent and disruptive. Instead, there is marked hyperactivity and impulsiveness, which may be verbal or physical. They may engage in physically dangerous activities without considering possible consequences. Violence toward others is usually in the form of accidents that occur in the course of playing with peers or other family members. In addition, these children are easily distracted, have difficulty cooperating in group situations and in following rules, and do not seem to listen to what is said to them.

Children with oppositional defiant disorder are often argumentative with adults, frequently lose their temper, and have low frustration tolerance. Later they may become heavy users of alcohol or illegal substances. They usually blame others for their own mistakes or problems. The degree of antisocial behavior by children with oppositional defiant disorder is not as serious as that for children with conduct disorder. Psychiatric disorders associated with violence are listed in Table 5.

■ LABORATORY AND OTHER DIAGNOSTIC TESTING

The routine laboratory tests done for psychiatric patients are indicated for violent patients. These include a complete blood count, blood chemistries including electrolytes, blood urea nitrogen, glucose, creatinine, calcium, phosphate, and liver function tests. In addition, routine tests of thyroid function, tests for syphilis, B_{12} folate levels, thiamine levels, urinalysis, electrocardiogram, and chest X rays comprise routine studies. If signs of substance abuse, intoxication, or withdrawal are suspected, then there should be a toxic screen of blood and urine as soon as possible to assay for alcohol, barbiturates, minor tranquilizers, amphetamines, cocaine, marijuana, hallucinogens, over-the-counter antihistamines, and anticholinergic drugs. Two types of assays should be done on each sample (e.g., radioimmunoassay

TABLE 5. **Other Psychiatric Disorders Posing Problems with Violence**

- Schizophrenia
- Delusional (paranoid) disorder
- Mania
- Personality disorders
    Organic personality syndrome
    Borderline personality
    Antisocial personality
- Mental retardation
- Disruptive behavior disorders
    Conduct disorders
    Attention-deficit hyperactivity disorder

and liquid or gas chromatography/mass spectrophotometry). Since cocaine has a very short half-life (i.e., one hour), it is essential that blood be drawn as soon as possible and that fluoride be added to prevent subsequent metabolism of cocaine in the tube. As these routine tests will uncover a number of the disorders listed in Tables 1 and 2, additional tests include human immunodeficiency virus (HIV) testing, glucose tolerance test, ceruloplasmin, urine porphobilinogen, heavy metal screening, antinuclear antibodies, serum and urine copper levels, and arterial blood gases. Lumbar puncture may be indicated for examination of the cerebrospinal fluid to assist in the diagnosis of central nervous system infection as well as multiple sclerosis. If there is raised intracranial pressure resulting from brain tumor, brain abscess, subdural hematoma, or intracerebral hemorrhage, then lumbar puncture is contraindicated.

I believe that the EEG should be part of the routine evaluation of the violent patient. The routine EEG should be augmented by nasopharyngeal leads as well as a sleep EEG.

Computed tomography and magnetic resonance imaging should be seriously considered for every evaluation of a violent patient. One or the other is essential for violent patients where an organic etiology is suspected because of confusion, dementia, disorientation and memory loss, history of alcohol or substance abuse, history of brain trauma, or history of seizures or other episodic behavioral disorders. Jaskiw et al. (3) compared computed tomography and magnetic resonance imaging. Magnetic resonance imaging is superior in terms of detecting pathology of the temporal lobe, apical areas, posteria fauca, and brain stem and is superior in detecting demyelinating disease. It does not expose the patient to ionizing radiation and can provide several imaging planes: traverse, sagittal, and coronal. Magnetic resonance imaging is limited because it is contraindicated with patients with metal surgical clips, metal skull plates, and cardiac pacemakers. The problem with magnetic resonance imaging, particularly for violent patients, is that it requires complete patient cooperation in terms of no movement. Computed tomography is superior in terms of its ability to detect intracranial calcifications, tumor margins, and old versus new hemorrhages. It does not require the same degree of patient cooperation and thus can be used for agitated, hyperactive patients better than magnetic resonance imaging.

In addition to detecting structural abnormalities of the brain, imaging can detect general atrophy, which is associated with a number of neurologic and medical illnesses themselves associated with violence. These include epilepsy, Wilson's disease, postencephalitic states, multiple sclerosis, Alzheimer's disease, multi-infarct dementia, head trauma, and system lupus erythematosus. Medical illnesses include nutritional deficiencies; Cushing's disease; and chronic intoxication with alcohol, solvents, and heavy metals (3). Laboratory tests and other diagnostic procedures for violent patients are listed in Table 6.

■ PSYCHOLOGICAL TESTING

I have found that a number of nonprojective psychological tests are useful for the evaluation of the violent patient. These include intelligence testing using the standard Wechsler Adult Intelligence Scale. As indicted previously, patients with subnormal intelligence can manifest violence as a result of their frustration and inability to communicate verbally their concerns and conflicts. The Bender-Gestalt is useful as a screening test for organic dysfunction. If the results are abnormal, the test can be followed by more complex batteries of tests (e.g., the Halstead-Reitan or the Luria-Nebraska).

There are scales that are specific for assessment of aggression and violence. These are used to measure baseline violence and subsequent violence in drug studies of treatment and other research on violent patients. The Buss-Durkee Hostility Inventory is a 75-item self-report questionnaire that measures aggressive behavior, irritability, negativism, suspicion, and verbal hostility (4). Yudofsky et al. (5) developed the Overt Aggression Scale, which can be used by staff to rate verbal aggression and physical aggression against the self, against other people, and against objects in relation to degree of seriousness, injury, or damage as well as duration, time, and types of intervention. A slightly modified version of this scale is presented in Figure 1. Brizer et al. (6) developed the Scale for Assessment of Aggressive and Agitated Behavior, which rates agitation, verbal assault, and assault against the self, others, or property in relation to severity, the

TABLE 6. **Laboratory Tests and Other Diagnostic Procedures for Violent Patients**

1. **Routine Assessment**
   - Complete blood count
   - Blood chemistries (electrolytes, blood urea nitrogen, glucose, creatinine, calcium, phosphate, and liver function tests)
   - Thyroid (T_3RU, T_4, thyroid-stimulating hormone)
   - Screening for syphilis
   - Vitamins (B_{12} folate, thiamine)
   - Urinalysis
   - Electrocardiogram
   - Chest X rays
   - Drug and alcohol screen of blood and urine (for drugs: radioimmunoassay, followed by gas chromatography/mass spectrophotometry if positive)
   - Electroencephalogram (nasopharyngeal leads and with sleep)
   - Bender-Gestalt
2. **Additional Tests Based on Clinical Suspicion**
   - Arterial blood gases (hypoxia)
   - HIV antibodies (AIDS, ARC)
   - Glucose tolerance test (hypoglycemia)
   - Ceruloplasmin, copper levels in urine and serum (Wilson's disease)
   - Urine porphobilinogen (porphyria)
   - Heavy metal screening (poisoning)
   - Antinuclear antibodies (systemic lupus erythematosus)
   - Lumbar puncture if intracranial pressure not elevated (infection, multiple sclerosis, hemorrhage)
   - Magnetic resonance imaging and/or computed tomography (tumors, hemorrhage, atrophy associated with epilepsy, Alzheimer's disease, multi-infarct dementia, head trauma, postencephalitic states, Wilson's disease, lupus, nutritional deficiencies, chronic alcoholism, solvents and heavy metals)
   - Psychological tests (intelligence tests, Halstead-Reitan, Luria-Nebraska)
   - Rating scales for assessment of aggression and violence (Buss-Durkee Hostility Inventory, Overt Aggression Scale, Scale for the Assessment of Aggressive and Agitated Behaviors)

initiator and target of aggression, level of agitation of other patients on the ward at the time of the incident, and intervention by staff. For purposes of behavioral treatment or to determine the

FIGURE 1. **The Overt Aggression Scale**

Name of Patient _____ Name of Rater _____
Sex of Patient _____ Date _____ Shift _____

Aggressive Behavior (check all that apply)

Verbal Aggression
___ Makes loud noises, shouts angrily
___ Yells mild personal insults (e.g., "You're stupid")
___ Curses viciously, uses foul language in anger, makes moderate threats to others or self
___ Makes clear threats of violence toward others or self (e.g., "I'm going to kill you") or requests help to control self

Physical Aggression Against Objects
___ Slams door, scatters clothing, makes a mess
___ Throws objects down, kicks furniture without breaking it, marks the wall
___ Breaks objects, smashes windows
___ Sets fires, throws objects dangerously

Physical Aggression Against Self
___ Picks or scratches skin, hits self, pulls hair (with no or minor head injury only)
___ Bangs heads, hits fist into objects, throws self onto floor or into objects (hurts self without serious injury)
___ Small cuts or bruises, minor burns
___ Mutilates self, makes deep cuts, bites that bleed, internal injury, fracture, loss of consciousness, loss of teeth

Physical Aggression Against Other People
___ Makes threatening gestures, swings at people, grabs at clothes
___ Strikes, kicks, pushes, pulls hair (without injury to them)
___ Attacks others, causing mild or moderate physical injury (bruises, sprain, welts)
___ Attacks others, causing severe physical injury (broken bones, deep lacerations, internal injury)

Time incident began: _____ Duration: _____

Intervention:

Note. Adapted from Yudofsky et al. (5).

effect of medication on aggression and violent behavior, the clinician can use these scales or devise specific observational categories (e.g., kicks others, bites others, punches others) that can be recorded in relation to frequency of such behaviors.

■ REFERENCES

1. Tardiff K: Determinants of human violence, in The American Psychiatric Association Annual Review, vol 6. Edited by Hales R, Frances AJ. Washington, DC, American Psychiatric Press, 1987
2. American Psychiatric Association: Diagnostic and Statistical Manual of Mental Disorders, 3rd ed, revised. Washington, DC, American Psychiatric Association, 1987
3. Jaskiw GE, Andreasen NC, Weinberger DR: X-ray computed tomography and magnetic resonance imaging in psychiatry, in The American Psychiatric Association Annual Review, vol 6. Edited by Hales R, Frances AJ. Washington, DC, American Psychiatric Press, 1987
4. Edmunds G, Kendrick DC: The Measurement of Human Aggression. Chichester, England, Ellis Horwood, 1980
5. Yudofsky SC, Silver JM, Jackson W, et al: The Overt Aggression Scale for the objective rating of verbal and physical aggression. Am J Psychiatry 1986; 143:35–39
6. Brizer DA, Convit A, Krakowski M, et al: A rating scale for reporting violence on psychiatric wards. Hosp Community Psychiatry 1987; 38:769–770

LONG-TERM MEDICATION 7

There is no one drug for treatment of violence because the underlying etiology for violence differs among patients. I will describe drugs that have some proven efficacy in the management of violent behavior, the types of patients in whom these medications have been most effective, dose and route of administration, and side effects.

■ NEUROLEPTICS

Table 1 lists the doses of neuroleptic medication recommended in non-emergency situations. The neuroleptics are antipsychotic medications used for schizophrenia and mania, and in some organic disorders for delusional thinking or control of violence. Neuroleptics are used as long-term medication primarily for schizophrenics. Especially for paranoid schizophrenics who have manifested violent behavior or made threats of violence, compliance with medication is notoriously bad. Thus clinicians should consider the use of long-acting depot forms of neuroleptic medication. Neuroleptic medication should not be used for violent mentally retarded patients unless psychotic symptomatology

TABLE 1. **Doses of Neuroleptic Medications Recommended in Nonemergency Situations**

1. **Haloperidol**[a]
   A. Haloperidol 0.5 to 2 mg by mouth for moderate symptoms and 3 to 5 mg by mouth for severe symptoms every 8 to 12 hours until psychosis is controlled. Maximum of 15 mg/day rarely need be exceeded. Maintenance dose rarely exceeds 8 mg/day. In chronic schizophrenia, higher doses may be needed, to a maximum of 100 mg/day until psychosis is controlled; maintenance dose rarely exceeds 20 mg/day.
   B. Haloperidol decanoate 25 to 100 mg im every three to five weeks. Initial dose is 10 to 15 times oral dose but not to exceed 100 mg (2 ml).
2. **Fluphenazine**
   Fluphenazine decanoate or enanthate 12.5 to 50 mg im every one to three weeks. Initial dose is 12.5 mg to be followed by 25 mg every two to three weeks until maintenance level but not to exceed 100 mg.
3. **Chlorpromazine**[a]
   Chlorpromazine 25 to 100 mg by mouth every one to four hours until psychotic symptoms are controlled. Dose rarely needs to exceed 1 g/day. Maintenance dose ranges from 300 to 800 mg/day. For severe psychosis, chlorpromazine 200 mg by mouth every four hours until psychotic symptoms are controlled.

Note. Doses should be adjusted based on the patient's age, weight, debilitation, and other clinical considerations.

[a]Neuroleptics other than haloperidol and chlorpromazine may be used in doses relative to the ones recommended here.

is part of the clinical picture. The use of long-term neuroleptics for these patients raises the risk of side effects (e.g., tardive dyskinesia) and the concern that learning may be impaired in this group of patients for whom learning is already a major problem.

Haloperidol or fluphenazine are popular because of their ability to be administered rapidly in high doses on inpatient units with minimal side effects, and with safety in terms of not decreasing the seizure threshold in epileptic patients. This is important in cases where subictal activity may coexist with schizophrenia. Of equal importance to combat noncompliance with haloperidol decanoate and fluphenazine decanoate or enanthate, there is a smooth transition from its use in the emergency situation to oral maintenance levels to long-term depot use.

In non-emergency situations for psychotic adult patients, haloperidol should be given 0.5 to 2 mg by mouth for moderate symptoms and 3 to 5 mg by mouth for severe symptoms every eight to 12 hours until psychotic symptoms are controlled. Doses above 15 mg/day are seldom required. When control has been achieved, the dose is lowered to a minimum effective dose, usually no more than 8 mg/day. Elderly or debilitated patients should be given 0.5 to 2 mg initially, with gradual increments of 0.5 mg. In chronic schizophrenics, higher doses are usually needed for active psychosis, starting with 6 to 15 mg/day in divided doses, with gradual increases until control is achieved. More than 100 mg/day is rarely needed; following control of psychotic symptoms, the dose should be decreased to maintenance levels, usually 15 to 20 mg/day (1).

Given the frequency of noncompliance and the dire consequences (i.e., renewed violent behavior by schizophrenics), serious thought should be given to the use of long-acting depot medication. The *Drug Evaluations* (1) recommend that the initial dose of haloperidol decanoate should be based on the patient's history, physical condition, and response to antipsychotic therapy. Small doses should be given initially, and the amount increased as needed. The initial dose of haloperidol decanoate should be 10 to 15 times the previous daily dose in oral haloperidol equivalents, but no more than a maximum initial dose of 100 mg (2 ml) should be given. Usually haloperidol decanoate has been effective when administered at monthly intervals; however, a variation in patient response may cause the clinician to adjust the interval as well as the dose. Lower initial and more gradual adjustment are required for elderly or debilitated patients. Monthly doses greater than 300 mg (6 ml) are rarely, if ever, indicated.

Fluphenazine should be given to adult psychotic patients, initially 2.5 to 10 mg/day by mouth and, when symptoms are controlled, be reduced to a maintenance level of 1 to 5 mg/day. Elderly or debilitated patients should be given 1 to 2.5 mg/day. The depot fluphenazine preparations should be given to adults initially at 12.5 mg to be followed by 25 mg every two to three weeks. The maintenance dose depends on the individual patient but the dose should not exceed 100 mg every two to three weeks. Elderly or debilitated patients should be started at 2.5 mg followed by 2.5 to 5 mg every two weeks.

If the clinician wishes to choose a neuroleptic with more sedative side effects or if extrapyramidal side effects are problematic, chlorpromazine or other low-potency neuroleptics are recommended. I do not recommend thioridizine for violent psychotic patients because the clinician may want to use propranolol for these patients, and, as will be discussed later, propranolol increases blood levels of thioridizine and the risk of pigmentary retinopathy. For psychosis, chlorpromazine should be given to adults 25 to 100 mg by mouth every one to four hours until control of psychotic symptoms has been achieved. Patients with severe psychosis, especially chronic schizophrenia, may require higher initial doses, around 200 mg by mouth every four hours. Daily doses exceeding 1 g are rarely needed. Elderly or debilitated patients should be given chlorpromazine at the lower range. If the patients have been at the optimal dose for two weeks, the amount should be reduced gradually to a minimum effective dose for maintenance. The average dose for patients under the age of 40 years is 300 to 800 mg/day. Elderly or debilitated patients require one-third to one-half the usual adult dose.

If compliance is a problem and depot medication is not indicated or desired, then blood levels of neuroleptics should be monitored to see if any drug is present. Analytical methods preferred are gas chromatography with mass spectrophotometry, as well as high pressure liquid chromatography for measurement of plasma concentrations.

The neuroleptic medications can produce a wide range of adverse side effects, which will be briefly described. Sedation is often found with the low-potency phenothiazines and may be desired for violent patients. If this becomes problematic, the single dose can be given at bedtime, and this will minimize daytime sedation.

Extrapyramidal reactions are more common with the high-potency neuroleptic medications. Those that occur early during treatment, usually within weeks, are those of acute dystonia, akathisia, and parkinsonism. Tardive dyskinesia usually occurs after months to years of treatment and occurs with both low- and high-potency neuroleptic medications.

Dystonic reactions most frequently occur following parenteral administration of neuroleptics. Acute dystonia appears usually within a few days of treatment and is characterized by abnormal, sustained posturing movements of the neck, jaw, trunk, and eyes, with protrusion of the tongue, spasms of the jaw, and extreme lateral upward gaze of the eyes. It is treated effectively and rapidly by anticholinergic medication, such as benztropine 1 to 2 mg im or iv or diphenhydramine 25 to 50 mg im. These medications may then be continued by oral administration following the resolution of the acute dystonic reaction.

Akathisia is manifested by a feeling of restlessness, usually in the lower extremities, and an urge to pace up and down. It appears within weeks to a few months after the beginning of neuroleptic medication. The agitation may be interpreted as aggression and violence, thus resulting in increased administration of neuroleptics and a vicious cycle of further agitation. The clinician should consider reducing the dose if akathisia occurs or administering an anticholinergic medication such as benztropine. Propranolol 10 to 60 mg/day can also be used to treat the akathisia. Propranolol at these doses has little effect in terms of aggression per se. To treat aggression, it must be used at much higher doses.

Parkinsonian symptoms are manifested by rigidity, slowness of movement, shuffling gait, a mask-like facies, and tremor resembling that of Parkinson's disease. Parkinsonian symptoms occur within weeks or a few months after neuroleptic medication has begun. The use of an anticholinergic drug such as benztropine is indicated for .5 mg by mouth three times a day. Amantadine can also be used for parkinsonian symptoms resulting from neuroleptics, 100 mg by mouth twice a day. Propranolol is given by mouth 20 mg three times a day. The recommended dose for diphenhydramine is 25 mg by mouth four times a day.

Akinesia is manifested by diminished spontaneity, few gestures, unspontaneous speech, apathy, and difficulty with initiating activities. As with parkinsonian symptoms, it can be managed by anticholinergic drugs as well as amantadine. The doses are similar to those used in parkinsonian symptoms and extrapyramidal side effects mentioned.

Tardive dyskinesia is characterized by choreiform movements of the face, jaw, tongue, trunk, and extremities. These are involuntary movements that are rapid, or purposeless and irregular or slow, or complex and irregular. Other involuntary movements of the lower legs, knees, and ankles include lateral knee movements and foot tapping. Involuntary movements of the neck, shoulders, and hip are those of rocking, twisting, or pelvic gyrations. Movements of the mouth and face include smacking, puckering, or pouting movements of the lips, involuntary biting, chewing, movements of the jaw, or clenching of the teeth. The tongue is involuntarily protruded or there may be tremors or chorioathetoid movements of the tongue. Tardive dyskinesia, like other dyskinesias, disappears during sleep and worsens with heightened arousal or anxiety. The elderly and female patients seem to be at increased risk of tardive dyskinesia.

Symptoms of tardive dyskinesia may be aggravated by the abrupt discontinuation of antipsychotic drugs and persist long after these medications have been withdrawn. Most patients improve within months; others require a year or more to improve after the neuroleptic medication is discontinued. Because drugs used to treat tardive dyskinesia are inadequate, prevention of the disorder is recommended. This is achieved by using neuroleptic medications for the treatment of acute psychosis for as short a period of time as is possible. If chronic medication is necessary, the patient's neuroleptic medication should be reduced at least once a year by 10 percent every three to seven days until the drug has been stopped completely or the patient's psychosis worsens. In general, *Drug Evaluations* (1) does not recommend any one drug treatment of tardive dyskinesia as being effective. If disabling tardive dyskinesia continues for years after the neuroleptic medication has been withdrawn, a number of drugs may be tried. These include bromocriptine and levodopa.

Neuroleptic malignant syndrome is a rare reaction and is characterized by severe muscular hypertonicity and akinesia, dysarthria, and fluctuating levels of consciousness, which can also include stupor and mutism. There is a high fever and various autonomic disturbances of heart rate and blood pressure. Accompanying it may be physical exhaustion, dehydration, and pneumonia or pulmonary emboli. The neuroleptic medication should be discontinued immediately, and supportive therapy such as control of fever and intravenous fluids should be given. There is some evidence that bromocriptine is effective in doses of 10 to 50 mg/day. Other drugs that have been used include amantadine and a combination of dantrolene and bromocriptine (1).

Autonomic nervous system side effects include orthostatic hypotension. Patients with this side effect should be told to stand slowly and carefully. If hypotension is severe, intravenous fluid should be given with norepinephine or phenylephrine (1). Additional autonomic side effects with neuroleptic medications, particularly thioridazine, include inhibition of ejaculation, dryness of mouth, blurred vision, tachycardia, urinary retention, and constipation. In elderly patients, adynamic ileus or severe urinary retention may occur, particularly if the neuroleptic medications are given concurrently with other anticholinergic drugs.

Hormonal side effects include delayed ovulation and menstruation, amenorrhea, and galactorrhea in women as well as gynecomastia in men. Some patients report loss of libido or inability to achieve orgasm. For men there have also been problems reported with erection.

There may be cardiac side effects, particularly with thioridizine. The electrocardiogram changes include prolonged QT interval and the appearance of U-waves.

Pigmentary retinopathy has been reported, particularly with thioridizine in doses greater than 800 mg/day and when large doses of chlorpromazine are used for long periods of time. The clinician should be particularly cautious with the concurrent use of propranolol because propranolol increases blood levels of thioridizine and other neuroleptic medications.

Side effects concerning the blood include agranulocytosis, which is very rare and occurs within the first three months of treatment. This is characterized by the appearance of a high fever, sore throat, and other signs of infection. It is usually associated with the phenothiazines and is often fatal. Phenothiazines should be discontinued immediately, and the infection should be treated. Agranulocytosis should be distinguished from a gradual decrease in white blood cells, which is usually not serious.

Allergic effects include jaundice, particularly with the phenothiazines, usually occurring in the first few weeks of treatment. The drug should be immediately discontinued. Various rashes have been reported infrequently; serious side effects such as exfoliative dermatitis are rare. When they appear, the drug should be discontinued immediately. Patients on neuroleptic medications are very sensitive to the sun and will develop severe sunburns or rashes. Patients should be advised to avoid exposure to sun and, if exposure is necessary, to use sunscreen lotions.

■ ANXIOLYTIC DRUGS AND SEDATIVES

The use of anxiolytic drugs and sedatives for the control of violence over a long period of time is generally not recommended. This stems from a concern that long-term use of these medications will result in drug abuse, dependency, and tolerance. In addition, they can produce sedation, confusion, and depression. A new drug, buspirone, has been shown as effective as diazepam and other benzodiazepines in managing anxiety. It appears to lack the hypnotic, anticonvulsant, and abuse potential of other antianxiety agents. It does not appear to interact with other sedating drugs, including alcohol. Recommended doses range from 15 to 30 mg/day, beginning with a dose of 5 mg three times a day and increasing by 5 mg every two to three days. The maximum dose recommended is 60 mg/day.

There should be clear-cut indications (e.g., anxiety) for the long-term use of anxiolytic agents. This is in distinction to their short-term emergency use, where sedative side effects are sought in the management of violence.

The side effects for the antianxiety agents and sedatives other than buspirone include sedation, impairment of motor ability, dizziness, and ataxia. Some patients have complained of blurred vision, diplopia, hypotension, amnesia, slurred speech, tremor, urinary incontinence, and constipation. The use of benzodiazepines during the first trimester of pregnancy has been reported to produce developmental abnormalities, including cleft lip with or without cleft palate.

The main side effect associated with anxiolytic agents and sedatives, particularly in patients with a history of violence and personality disorders, is that of abuse and dependence. Physical dependence results in a withdrawal reaction if these medications are discontinued rapidly. This withdrawal reaction may involve aggression and violent behavior as well as other symptoms such as anxiety, irritability, insomnia, tremors, headache, dizziness, anorexia, nausea, vomiting, diarrhea, incoordination, seizures, and depression. The onset of the withdrawal reaction depends on the particular medication and may be anywhere from a day for a short-acting drug such as lorazepam up to one week following cessation of other longer-acting drugs. A gradual reduction of dosage is recommended, namely 5 to 10 percent a day for 10 to 14 days (1). A long-acting benzodiazepine may be substituted for shorter-acting benzodiazepines. Patients with a history of seizures, alcohol abuse, or abuse of other drugs should be hospitalized for detoxification.

■ CARBAMAZEPINE AND OTHER ANTICONVULSANTS

Table 2 summarizes the use of carbamazepine in the management of violent behavior. Carbamazepine is approved as an anticonvulsant medication for complex partial seizures as well as generalized clonic-tonic seizures and other types of partial seizures. Although it is not recommended as the anticonvulsant of first choice, it is very popular due to fewer side effects, such as sedation, when compared to phenytoin and barbiturates (2).

There have been a number of case studies and open drug trials that have indicated that carbamazepine is probably effective for the management of aggression in a number of different types of psychiatric patients. In a double-blind, crossover study of 13 chronic psychiatric patients, 10 of whom were schizophrenic, Neppe (3) reported beneficial effects in terms of decreasing aggressive episodes. Although the patients were not epileptic, they did have temporal lobe electroencephalogram (EEG) abnormalities. The patients were treated with neuroleptics, anticholinergics, antidepressants, and benzodiazepines. The dose of carba-

TABLE 2. **Use of Carbamazepine in the Management of Violent Behavior**

---

1. Indications include:
   A. Complex partial seizures and other seizures.
   B. Schizophrenics with or without electroencephalogram abnormalities (with concurrent neuroleptic medication).
   C. Other patients with episodic violence who do not have gross brain damage.
2. Laboratory testing:
   A. Complete blood count and platelet count before treatment and every two weeks for the first two months and every three months thereafter.
   B. Liver function tests (SGOT, SGPT, LDH, and alkaline phosphatase) before treatment, every month early in treatment, and every three months thereafter.
   C. Patients with leukopenia, thrombocytopenia, or liver disease should not be treated with carbamazepine.
3. Patients with seizures require higher doses than patients without seizures. Initially carbamazepine 100 to 200 mg twice daily for one week and then increase by 100- to 200-mg increments; measure serum levels daily. For seizure control, up to 1,200 mg/day may be needed. For other patients, lower doses, approximately 600 mg/day are needed.
4. Recommended therapeutic serum levels range from 4 to 12 ng/ml. Once response is achieved and therapeutic level reached, blood levels should be monitored every month for the first three months and every three months thereafter.

Note. SGOT = serum glutamic-oxaloacetic transaminase; SGPT = serum glutamic-pyruvic transaminase; LDH = lactate dehydrogenase.

mazepine was 200 mg three times a day. Luchins (4) reported on an open carbamazepine trial in seven chronic psychiatric inpatients, six of whom were schizophrenics. None of the patients had EEG abnormalities. He reported that six of the seven patients had fewer aggressive episodes on carbamazepine than either before or after the drug. All the patients were concurrently treated with neuroleptic drugs. Mattes et al. (5) found that carbamazepine is very effective in decreasing aggression in patients with psychiatric diagnoses other than schizophrenia. These include personality disorders, conduct disorders, and some organic disorders. Caution should be given to the use of carbamazepine in patients with gross brain damage or mental retardation because there have been reports of paradoxical worsening of aggression in this group of patients.

In conclusion, there is some evidence that carbamazepine may be effective in terms of managing aggression and irritability in patients with overt seizures, both complex partial seizures and generalized seizures; in schizophrenic patients with and without EEG abnormalities; and with other types of patients with episodic violence without gross brain damage or mental retardation.

Early reports about carbamazepine causing thrombocytopenia, agranulocytosis, and aplastic anemia have not been supported, and these side effects appear to be rare. Nevertheless, monitoring of hematologic and liver functioning is essential in addition to a complete medical evaluation. Complete blood count and platelet count are recommended before treatment and every two weeks for the first two months of treatment and every three months thereafter. Liver functioning tests should include serum glutamic-oxaloacetic transaminase (SGOT), serum glutamic-pyruvic transaminase (SGPT), lactate dehydrogenase (LDH), and alkaline phosphatase. These tests should be repeated every month early in treatment and every three months thereafter. Patients with leukopenia, thrombocytopenia, or liver disease should not be treated with carbamazepine (6).

Some patients treated with carbamazepine report side effects such as nausea, drowsiness, vertigo, ataxia, blurred vision, and diplopia, which are usually mild and decrease when the dosages decrease. There are other less frequent toxic consequences of treatment such as jaundice, renal effects, nystagmus, skin reactions, and thyroid effects. In approximately 5 percent of patients, carbamazepine is discontinued due to toxic reactions. Dyskinetic movements such as dystonia, dyskinesias, and other extrapyramidal reactions are rare and self-limited if the medication is withdrawn or the dosage decreased.

For an anticonvulsant response with carbamazepine, the therapeutic serum levels are from 4 to 12 ng/ml. The usual method for treatment of seizures is to prescribe 100 to 200 mg twice a day for one week, and then to increase the dose by 100- to 200-mg increments and to measure serum levels when daily doses of 400 to 600 mg are achieved. It is not uncommon for patients with seizure disorders to take up to 1,200 mg/day. The onset of therapeutic effects is within the first days or weeks after treatment is initiated (2).

Patients without seizure disorders have benefited from carbamazepine at doses of approximately 600 mg/day. Once the therapeutic level is reached and a response is obtained, blood levels of carbamazepine should be monitored every month for the first three months and then every three months thereafter.

Other anticonvulsants have been tried in the control of aggression with inconsistent results (7). Positive findings have included the use of diphenylhydantoin in the treatment of aggressive mentally retarded children, violent nonepileptic male adults (half of whom had EEG abnormalities), and adults with episodic dyscontrol syndrome. Negative results with diphenylhydantoin have included the treatment of aggression in criminal offenders or aggressive delinquent boys. One study found that half of aggressive chronic schizophrenics responded to primidone; another study found ethosuximide useful for patients with episodic dyscontrol, abnormal EEGs, and history of organic impairment.

■ PROPRANOLOL AND OTHER BETA BLOCKERS

Table 3 lists the use of propranolol in the management of violent behavior. Silver and Yudofsky (8) reviewed a number of control studies, open trials, and case reports on the effectiveness of propranolol in the management of aggressive behavior. Most of the patients studied and responding to propranolol were those with organic brain disease, often with gross impairment secondary to trauma, tumor, alcoholism, encephalitis, Huntington's disease, dementia, Wilson's disease, Korsakoff's psychosis, and mental retardation. In addition, some patients with minimal brain dysfunction or attention deficit have also been reported to respond to propranolol. Nearly all the patients in these studies were refractory to other medications, including neuroleptics, anxiolytic agents, anticonvulsants, and lithium. In a number of cases, concurrent neuroleptic medication was used.

Before using propranolol, there should be a thorough medical evaluation of the patient. Patients with the following diseases should be excluded from treatment with propranolol: bronchial

TABLE 3. **Use of Propranolol in the Management of Violent Behavior**

1. Primary indications include violent patients with gross brain impairment with or without other psychiatric disorders.
2. Contraindications include patients with bronchial asthma, chronic obstructive pulmonary disease, insulin-dependent diabetes, cardiac diseases including angina or congestive heart failure, diabetes mellitus, significant peripheral vascular disease, severe renal disease, or hyperthyroidism. Sudden discontinuation of propranolol in hyperactive patients may result in rebound hypertension.
3. Initially propranolol is given 20 mg three times a day and is increased by 60 mg every three to four days. A test dose of 20 mg may be given if there are concerns about hypotension or bradycardia.
4. Propranolol is increased unless pulse rate falls below 50 beats per minute or if systolic blood pressure is below 90 mm Hg. Propranolol should be held or decreased if severe dizziness, ataxia, or wheezing occurs.
5. Daily doses greater than 800 mg are rarely needed for control of violent behavior.
6. Although therapeutic effect may be seen in several days, patient should be maintained on highest dose possible for at least eight weeks before calling the drug trial a failure.
7. Discontinuation of propranolol should be gradual, with decreases of 60 mg/day until the patient is on 60 mg/day. After that the dose should be decreased by 20 mg every other day.
8. If patient is on neuroleptics or anticonvulsants, blood levels of these medications, particularly thioridizine, should be monitored.

asthma, chronic obstructive pulmonary disease, insulin-dependent diabetes, cardiac diseases including angina or congestive heart failure, diabetes mellitus, significant peripheral vascular disease, severe renal disease, and hyperthyroidism. Hypertensive patients should be given propranolol with caution because sudden discontinuation of propranolol may result in rebound hypertension.

The initial dose of propranolol is 20 mg three times a day, which is increased by 60 mg every three to four days. A test dose of 20 mg may be given if there are clinical concerns about hypotension or bradycardia. Propranolol is increased unless the pulse rate is reduced below 50 beats per minute or if the systolic blood pressure is less than 90 mm Hg. If the patient experiences severe dizziness, ataxia, or wheezing, the medication should be held and then reduced or discontinued if the symptoms persist. Doses of greater than 800 mg are usually not required to control aggressive behavior. Although a therapeutic effect may be seen in several days, it usually takes longer. The patient should be maintained on the highest dose of propranolol for at least eight weeks before determining that the patient is not responding to the medication. If the patient is on neuroleptic medication or anticonvulsant medication, plasma blood levels of neuroleptics should be monitored carefully. Propranolol has been shown to increase plasma blood levels of neuroleptic medications, particularly thioridizine, which could result in pigmentary retinopathy.

To withdraw the patient from propranolol, it should be decreased gradually by 60 mg/day until the patient is on a daily dose of 60 mg/day. Then the medication should be decreased at the rate of 20 mg every other day. Propranolol should be decreased even more gradually in patients with hypertension to prevent rebound hypertension.

Side effects found with propranolol include hypotension and bradycardia, although these may be managed by decreasing the dose of the drug. Above 300 mg/day there is usually no worsening of bradycardia or hypotension. Depression has been reported rarely by patients receiving propranolol; sedation is sometimes reported as a side effect.

Silver and Yudofsky (8) reviewed other case studies using beta blockers other than propranolol. These include the use of nadolol in doses of 80 to 160 mg/day in the treatment of aggressive patients with chronic paranoid schizophrenia. Pindolol has been reported to be effective in the treatment of aggression in patients with organic brain syndrome. Metoprolol has been reported effective with two patients: one with intermittent explosive disorder related to meningitis and alcohol abuse, and the other with a penetrating brain trauma with temporal lobe epilepsy. The control of aggressive outbursts was reported with metoprolol 200 to 300 mg/day.

■ LITHIUM

Table 4 lists the use of lithium in the management of violent patients. Long-term use of lithium helps to prevent manic episodes and associated hyperactive aggressive behavior. The use of lithium for disorders other than bipolar disorders for the management of aggression has been much more controversial. In a double-blind trial testing the effectiveness of lithium in the treatment of aggression in adult mentally retarded patients, Craft et al. (9) found that 73 percent of patients showed a reduction in aggression during treatment. A serum lithium concentration of 0.7 to 1.0 mmol/liter was necessary for a clinical effect. The use of lithium was the same as that for the management of bipolar patients. Although there have been other reports of the use of lithium in other disorders, there is a sparsity of double-blind controlled studies. These disorders include patients with organic brain syndrome or head injury; aggressive schizophrenics; nonpsychotic, aggressive prisoners; and delinquents and children with conduct or attention-deficit hyperactivity disorders. There have been some who contend that lithium can increase interictal aggression in patients with temporal lobe epilepsy and cause other adverse effects in patients with other seizure disorders and other abnormal EEG changes.

Since lithium affects many organ systems in the body, an extensive medical examination is recommended prior to beginning lithium and during the course of treatment (6). The medical evaluation includes ascertaining whether there is a history of familial kidney disease and whether there are symptoms of certain disorders, particularly related to the kidney (i.e., diabetes mellitus, hypertension, and the use of medications or exposure to toxins which may affect the kidney). Laboratory evaluations should include blood urea nitrogen, creatine, creatine clearance (24-hour urine), electrolytes, urinalysis, 24-hour urine volume, and fluid deprivation test. The medical evaluation for thyroid disease should include family history of thyroid disease as well as eliciting current symptoms related to thyroid disease (e.g., goiter, thin hair). Laboratory evaluation should include T_3RU, T_4 radioimmunoassay, T_4I, thyroid-stimulating hormone, and antithyroid antibodies. Evaluation of hyperparathyroidism should include measurement of serum calcium. If the serum calcium is elevated, the patient should be referred for further evaluation. Evaluation of cardiac function should include a history of symptoms of cardiac disease and an electrocardiogram if the patient is over 40 years of age or if there is a suspicion of cardiac disease. In

TABLE 4. **Use of Lithium in the Management of Violent Patients**

---

1. Primary efficacy supported in violent patients with bipolar disorder or mental retardation. Other reports of efficacy in violent patients with organic brain syndrome or head injury, schizophrenia, nonpsychotic prisoners, and children with conduct or attention-deficit hyperactivity disorder.
2. Not recommended for aggression in patients with complex partial seizures, other seizures, or electroencephalogram abnormalities.
3. Medical examination and laboratory tests should rule out:
   A. Kidney disease (blood urea nitrogen, creatinine, creatinine clearance, electrolytes, urinalysis, 24-hr. urine volume)
   B. Thyroid disease (T_3RU, T_4 radioimmunoassay, T_4I, thyroid-stimulating hormone, and antithyroid antibodies)
   C. Parathyroid disease (serum calcium)
   D. Cardiac disease (electrocardiogram)
   E. Pregnancy (causes cardiac malformation in fetus)
   F. Diabetes mellitus (fasting blood sugar, urine ketones)
4. Most patients can start on 300 mg twice a day and the dose increased by 300 mg every three to four days.
5. Therapeutic plasma levels are 0.7 to 1.0 mEq/liter. Once level stabilizes, it should be monitored every month for the first six months and every two to three months afterward.

---

addition, a complete white blood cell count with differential should be ordered. Last, a fasting blood glucose and the presence of ketones in the urine should be assessed. Laboratory tests should be repeated every three to six months for renal and thyroid dysfunction, one month after serum level is stable, and every year thereafter for cardiac dysfunction. The fasting glucose level should be monitored every year.

The therapeutic plasma levels for patients on lithium to control aggression range from .7 to 1.0 mEq/liter. Most patients can be started on 300 mg twice a day of lithium carbonate; this dose can be increased by 300 mg every three to four days. Plasma levels should be obtained 12 hours after the last lithium dose. Once the therapeutic lithium level has been stabilized, levels should be monitored every month for the first six months and every two to three months afterward. Because congenital abnormalities, particularly heart defects, have been reported, lithium should not be used during pregnancy. It should be used with caution in women of childbearing age. Lithium should not be used in conjunction with iodine or medicines containing iodides (e.g., cough medicines, multivitamin preparations). Indomethacine and phenylbutazone have been shown to elevate serum lithium concentrations.

With serum lithium below toxic levels (which are 1.5 to 2.0 mEq/liter), transient mild to moderate side effects may occur. The most common reactions include nausea, diarrhea, malaise, and fine hand tremors. Other common effects reported are thirst, polyuria, polydipsia, and fatigue. Hand tremors may respond to low doses of propranolol.

As one approaches the toxic range of serum lithium levels, drowsiness, vomiting, muscle weakness, ataxia, dryness of mouth, abdominal pain, lethargy, dizziness, slurred speech, and nystagmus are early signs of intoxication. At levels above 2 mEq/liter, symptoms include anorexia, severe nausea and vomiting, blurred vision, fasciculations, clonic movements of the whole body and limbs, hyperactive tendon reflexes, choreoathetoid movements, toxic psychosis, syncope, EEG changes, acute circulatory failure, stupor, and coma. The last stages of lithium toxicity are manifested by generalized convulsions, oliguria, and death.

Long-term administration of lithium has resulted in impaired renal function and, rarely, persistent neurologic deficits. Thus long-term lithium treatment for violence should be embarked on after serious consideration. Since lithium is excreted by the kidneys, it should be used cautiously in patients receiving diuretics or those on low-salt diets. There should be precautions taken when lithium is used in the elderly because renal function usually declines with age. Leukocytosis has been reported, is usually not serious, and can be reversed with discontinuation of lithium treatment. If lithium is used concurrently with neuroleptic medications, blood levels of the neuroleptic medication should be monitored.

■ PSYCHOSTIMULANTS

Brizer (7) reviewed the literature on the use of psychostimulants for the treatment of violent behavior. The use of amphetamines is accepted in controlling aggressive behavior associated with attention-deficit hyperactivity disorder. There have been some reports of the successful use of amphetamines to control aggression in adults with a history of this disorder as well. In addition, there were two studies reporting the successful use of amphetamines in delinquent youths: one to control aggression in a group of hospitalized black aggressive delinquents, and the other to decrease violence in the classroom for a group of aggressive outpatient boys with antisocial behavior. Further studies are indicated, and the clinician should proceed with caution in prescribing amphetamines because there is great potential for addiction, abuse, and the production of violent behavior through hyperactivity, emotional lability, or delusional thinking as a result of abuse of psychostimulants.

■ TRYPTOPHAN

As noted in Chapter 2, research has pointed to an association of low levels of 5-hydroxyindoleacetic acid (5-HIAA) and aggressive, impulsive behavior in both externally directed violence and suicide. As a result, some researchers have attempted to increase serotonin levels through the administration of the precursors of serotonin such as the amino acid tryptophan. Brizer (7) reviewed the literature, including the successful use of tryptophan in a demented 82-year-old woman with agitation and self-destructive behavior. Two additional research studies have pointed to the successful use of tryptophan. One studied 12 aggressive schizophrenic offenders where tryptophan (4 to 8 g/day for four weeks) resulted in a decrease of assaultive incidents. The other study found that four of six patients (five of whom had neuroleptic-refractory aggression) showed moderate significant improvements in violent behavior while receiving trazodone (50 mg twice a day) plus tryptophan (500 mg twice a day) (7). Tryptophan is a relatively safe medication; its major side effects include nausea and sedation. Further studies are indicated to evaluate its usefulness in the management of impulsive violent behavior.

■ REFERENCES

1. American Medical Association: Drug Evaluations, 6th ed. Chicago, American Medical Association, 1986

2. Evans RW, Gualtieri CT: Carbamazepine: a neuropsychological and psychiatric profile. Clin Neuropharmacol 1985; 8:221–241

3. Neppe VM: Carbamazepine as adjunctive treatment in nonepileptic chronic inpatients with EEG temporal lobe abnormalities. J Clin Psychiatry 1981; 44:326–331

4. Luchins DI: Carbamazepine in psychiatric syndromes: clinical and neuropharmacological properties. Psychopharmacol Bull 1984; 20:569–571

5. Mattes JA, Rosenberg J, Mays D: Carbamazepine versus propranolol in patients with uncontrolled rage outbursts: a random assignment study. Psychopharmacol Bull 1984; 20:98–100

6. Silver JM, Yudofsky SC: Psychopharmacology and electroconvulsive therapy, in The American Psychiatric Press Textbook of Psychiatry. Edited by Talbott JA, Hales RE, Yudofsky SC. Washington, DC, American Psychiatric Press, 1988

7. Brizer DA: Psychopharmacology and the management of violent patients. Psychiatr Clin North Am 1988; 11:551–568

8. Silver JM, Yudofsky S: Propranolol for aggression: literature review and clinical guidelines. International Drug Newsletter 1985; 20:9–12

9. Craft M, Ismail IA, Krishnamurti D, et al: Lithium in the treatment of aggression in mentally handicapped patients. Br J Psychiatry 1987; 150:685–689

LONG-TERM PSYCHOTHERAPY 8

Long-term psychotherapy with violent patients is an activity that usually takes place in an outpatient setting and relies on an understanding of the dynamics of the individual's violence in the context of the environment. Long-term psychotherapy treatment of patients in hospitals differs from long-term psychotherapy of outpatients in that it is more likely behavioral therapy given to chronic severely impaired patients, most likely with a diagnosis of mental retardation or schizophrenia. An appreciation of the principles of behavioral therapy is given in Chapter 9.

The principles of psychotherapy outlined here have been taken from an article addressing the overall long-term treatment of the violent patient (1). The present chapter complements

Chapter 7 (on the use of long-term medication) because some of the patients receiving psychotherapy will be good candidates for medication as well.

Assaultive behavior is less frequently seen as a problem for patients presenting for outpatient treatment than for inpatient treatment. Of the patients presenting to the clinics at two private psychiatric hospitals in New York, 3 percent had manifested recent violence toward other persons (2). This is less than 10 percent of patients with a history of recent violence presenting to private and public hospitals for admission (3, 4).

Although, as with the admission studies, males are more likely than females and younger patients more likely than older patients to manifest violent behavior, diagnostic characteristics of violent outpatients differed from those of violent inpatients. Violent patients presenting to outpatient clinics were more likely to be in the nonpsychotic diagnostic categories (e.g., personality, child, or adolescence disorders) rather than psychotic disorders. Among violent psychiatric outpatients, the spouse, mate, or other family members were targets of violence in approximately 60 percent of the cases.

■ **TYPES OF PATIENTS**

Most outpatient treatment will involve psychotherapy with patients with personality disorders. Personality disorders such as the borderline type often display self-mutilation and temper outbursts; antisocial personalities are usually violent toward others, not themselves. The passive-aggressive personality may display anger; the weakening of control in the obsessive-compulsive personality may manifest itself in a violent outburst. Paranoid and narcissistic personalities may show outbursts of aggression when challenged; histrionic personalities as well may react to stress with dramatic shows of violence. Violence may be a prominent part of character pathology and form the basis for therapy; however, the best candidate for outpatient treatment is the patient with episodic violence who manifests remorse following these violent episodes.

■ TYPES OF PSYCHOTHERAPIES

Group and family therapies are the usual types of outpatient psychotherapy for the violent patient for several reasons. First, most violence goes on within families and thus to treat the patient in isolation is ineffective, particularly if the victim and patient are engaged in provocative interactions. This is also the case with violent adolescents who are within a family unit. Second, the group process often allows violent patients to discuss issues that they are too frightened to bring up in a one-to-one setting. When structured to treat the impulse character disorder, group therapy allows participants to see other patients troubled by recurring temper outbursts and low self-esteem. Since these patients frequently do not have the ability to see their own pathology, confrontation by other members of the group becomes more effective and less threatening than if done by the therapist.

■ GOALS OF PSYCHOTHERAPY

There are five major goals in the psychotherapy of the violent patient. First, the therapist must evaluate the motivation of the patient and the reasons for a request for psychotherapy and treatment. A reason such as wanting to impress the court in an impending trial for a violent offense is not as good a reason as remorse by the patient or pressure from a spouse considering divorce.

The second goal is the development of self-control. Often this is not difficult in the beginning phases of therapy. In the treatment of aggressive patients, there is often an initial "honeymoon" phase when aggression appears to cease. The therapist is endowed with attributes that represent the opposite of the patient's inner state. Accordingly, strength is obtained by contact with the therapist, and the patient finds the ability to function without becoming aggressive. Sooner or later, however, this relationship becomes tested, and the patient encounters some conflict outside of the treatment setting to which he or she responds with violence. Both the patient and the family are disappointed, and this is when the real work of psychotherapy begins.

Third, change in the nature of the transference is the most critical and potentially dangerous aspect of work with aggressive patients. The therapist must continually monitor this set of feelings because it can change as a function of the patient's primitiveness. Paranoid and borderline patients, or those with a history of psychotic illness, are prone to handle the intimacy of therapy with threats of violence or actual violent or destructive acts. Playful gestures within the therapy hour that suggest such rages should spark discussion, as should letters or notes or messages on answering machines that can be interpreted as threatening or indicative of aggressive thoughts on the part of the patient. The purchase of or keeping weapons at home should be naturally monitored; in the context of the transference, it should give the therapist pause for thought. The therapist must constantly assess whether the patient poses a danger to him or her.

The countertransference, likewise, requires evaluation (5). It is the most important indicator of the relationship between patient and therapist, although one easily subject to distortion in the case of violence. Aggression usually mobilizes fear in the clinician, who can respond by projecting anxieties onto the patient and seeing the latter as more violent and threatening than the patient really is. On the other hand, denial of fear can lead to the false perception of the patient as "interesting" instead of a potential danger to society. One way of guarding against such errors is to have the patient seen in consultation. Forensic institutions operate on the principle of shared responsibility whereby several clinicians make judgments about the patient's violent propensities. In clinical practice, the therapist should likewise think about having the violent patient seen from another viewpoint. This is particularly important when the clinician is excessively worried about the risks the patient poses to society, and when the clinician becomes frightened for his or her own safety. Consultation also has legal implications for the more formal assessment of risk, as will be described later.

The fourth goal of psychotherapy is to foster the development of affective awareness. It is critical for a violent patient to recognize when he or she is becoming angry so that the patient is neither flooded with affect or so little aware of it that the patient cannot respond appropriately to events. The patient must come to realize when he or she is getting angry and must identify the physiologic state of anger. Once the patient is aware of the anger, he or she can at least try and talk about it.

There should be the development of insight regarding the dynamics of violence for the individual patient and spouse, other family members, and friends. This involves creating some awareness within the patient by sensitization to the precipitating insults. This involves repeated attempts on the clinician's part to draw the patient's attention to issues of self-esteem and their challenge. The patient must develop insight into vulnerabilities, whether they be size, sexuality, abandonment, or other recurring themes. The clinician's role is always to inquire why the patient became aggressive in response to a perceived insult. A wife's provocative comment, a statement of ridicule by a fellow worker, or a sick child's relentless crying may variably evoke rage by kindling inner sensitivities defended against by violence. Weakness is a key dynamic in the violent patient, and long-term therapy must constantly focus on the violent patient as helpless. As the patient comes to grips with these inner frailties and accepts them, the patient will develop a greater tolerance with regard to human relationships and the self. This takes time.

The fifth goal of psychotherapy involves the elucidation of fantasy with the intent of increasing the patient's ability to predict and appreciate emotionally the sequelae of his or her acts. For example, a patient should come to realize that if he hits his wife, he may end up in jail. To this end, he must fantasize what it is like to end up in jail with its steel doors and concrete floors. "What would happen if . . . " is the method used to get patients to think about the outcome of their behaviors. This tactic is mundane, but crucial to a successful therapy. Anticipation of consequences is a powerful cognitive way to stop oneself from being violent.

Aspects of a patient's life outside the office setting must be considered to understand the dynamics of violence and to intervene as an advocate for the patient. These aspects may involve understanding that a patient with poor education lacks legitimate nonviolent means of achievement and helping the patient improve educationally (e.g., through vocational schooling). It may be necessary to intervene if the patient's employment is threatened. Consideration should be given to housing in terms of crowding and stress, the patient's subculture, peers, and neighborhood along the lines indicated in Chapter 2. If intervention is not warranted, at least therapy should be done, keeping in mind what patients are subjected to in the environment once they leave a session in one's office.

There are special concerns about the treatment of violent patients, particularly in an outpatient setting. There are countertransference and inappropriate reactions by the therapist, legitimate concerns about one's safety, and the responsibility under *Tarasoff*-like rulings to protect potential victims from violence by one's patients. Table 1 lists goals of outpatient psychotherapy with violent patients.

■ THERAPISTS' REACTIONS TO VIOLENT PATIENTS

As Lion and Pasternak (5) pointed out, it is natural to have anxiety that a violent patient will kill someone or to have exces-

TABLE 1. Goals of Outpatient Psychotherapy with the Violent Patient

- Evaluate the true reason or motivation of the patient to enter psychotherapy.
- Facilitate verbal expression of problems and conflicts in a nonjudgmental manner.
- Help the patient develop self-control.
- Help the patient deal with lapses of self-control so as not to jeopardize therapy.
- Monitor the nature of the transference, with particular emphasis on danger to the therapist.
- Monitor the nature of the countertransference with particular emphasis on the real danger a patient poses to the therapist and others.
- Foster the development of awareness of angry and hostile emotions and how they feel psychologically and physiologically.
- Foster the development of insight into the dynamics and escalation of violence in relation to other persons, particularly perceived or real challenges to self-esteem and vulnerabilities of the patient.
- Increase the patient's ability to appreciate emotionally the consequences of continued violence (e.g., jail or divorce).
- Assist with restructuring of the patient's environment to prevent violence.

sive concern about ourselves as victims. Thus it is important that the therapist analyze his or her reactions, particularly negative ones, to violent patients. As in other areas of psychiatry, it is not necessarily wrong to have negative or inappropriate reactions to patients, but it is wrong not to have insight about these and to act on them inappropriately. Therapists have experienced a wide variety of defense mechanisms in terms of violent patients (e.g., projection in terms of anger at a patient for lack of progress and exaggeration of the patient's violent potential). There may be defense mechanisms of displacement from one violent patient to another who may not pose a danger, as well as reaction formation or identification with the aggressor in terms of treating attractive patients who are viewed as not as dangerous when in fact they are.

Coupled with the need for alertness on the part of the therapist is the need to avoid denial. Questions need to be asked about the ownership of weapons; about the existence of a victim; about previous violence toward the victim; about the patient's attitudes toward his or her children, pets, and spouse; and about level of destructiveness within the household. When patients indicate that they lost their temper, they should be questioned in depth, lest both they and their therapist dismiss the event in mutual denial. This type of endeavor in the context of therapy may appear unpleasant, but it is critical to the successful outcome of treatment. Knowledge of violence is too easily suppressed in the service of liking and identifying with a patient or avoiding confrontation with the patient or the patient's anger. Table 2 lists some inappropriate reactions to violent patients by therapists.

TABLE 2. **Some Inappropriate Reactions to Violent Patients by Therapists**

- Projection of one's anger (e.g., about the lack of progress) and exaggeration of the patient's potential for violence.
- Displacement of concern about violence potential from one patient to another in a group.
- Reaction formation or identifying with an attractive patient and not accurately viewing the patient as being violent.
- Denial and failure to see the patient as being a serious threat for violence.

■ SAFETY

The clinician in an outpatient setting should establish the firmest contract regarding the patient's behavior. Most therapists practice in relative isolation, away from security personnel and other institutional safeguards, and thus must carefully screen their patients' ability to be manageable. Patients who have shown a capacity to be violent should be assessed for their capacity to tolerate verbal exploration in an office setting without agitation. The strictest limits should be set on the use of disinhibiting agents such as alcohol prior to an office visit. If a crisis occurs, the therapist might wish to consider seeing the patient in the emergency room or in a setting where safety can be monitored and help is available. Here appropriate intervention can be made in the matter of hospitalization, and an assessment can be made regarding the role of the victim.

The safety of the office in the outpatient setting merits consideration. There should be a means of communicating both ways in case of trouble (i.e., for the receptionist to inform the therapist and the therapist to inform the outside staff of problems with violent patients). If the receptionist senses that the patient poses a threat (e.g., appears agitated, angry, or has been drinking), this should be communicated to the therapist before the therapist and patient enter the office and close the door. This may be done by code words or some other prearranged signal. Likewise, if the therapist is in danger inside the office (e.g., from a patient who is becoming threatening or one who perhaps produces a weapon), then the therapist should be able, through a code word by telephone or even a buzzer system, to alert the staff outside the office of the situation. The safety of the therapist is a prime consideration because even feeling unsafe will impair evaluation and treatment.

A more subtle aspect of ensuring the safety of the therapist is the response to a threat made by a patient. There is no such thing as a harmless threat, and clinicians threatened by former patients or those in active therapy must respond. Threats will not go away. A therapist must demand to meet with the threatening patient in a safe place, with colleagues or security personnel available and alerted. The therapist can state that the threats are frightening, but that the therapist wishes to resolve what is going on between himself or herself and the patient. It is permissible—indeed, therapeutic—for a clinician to admit fear to a patient because the latter is utilizing the very threat to create an aura of strength and power. At the same time, however, the appropriate comment about the threat involves some acknowledgment about its illegality and the response the therapist will take. Violent patients who make verbal threats wish for intervention, and controls furnish this intervention. Table 3 provides guidelines for therapist safety in psychotherapy.

■ DUTY TO PROTECT INTENDED VICTIMS

A therapist has a duty to protect intended victims of violence by one's patients. The *Tarasoff* ruling in California and subsequent *Tarasoff*-like decisions will be discussed in Chapter 11. In addition, a model for the prediction of short-term violent potential will be discussed in Chapter 10. Here, however, some other clinical aspects of this responsibility will be addressed. A prime conflict in the duty to protect intended victims is the violation of confidentiality versus the need to inform an intended victim of a real risk. Generally speaking, the therapist who decides that a patient is genuinely dangerous to a specific person is under some legal pressure to intervene, even though such intervention can include, for example, a period of hospitalization. To adopt a rigid position of informing all intended victims is to render a disservice to both the patient and intended victim. One tries, in all instances, to work the problem through in some therapeutic manner. Thus the therapist can tell the patient that he or she is concerned about

TABLE 3. **Safety of the Therapist in Psychotherapy**

- Monitor transference.
- Know one's self and countertransference.
- See patients in a non-isolated office setting.
- Set strict limits on the patient's use of alcohol or drugs before sessions.
- Devise a method of warning from receptionist to therapist and vice versa if patient is a threat.
- Take all verbal threats from patients seriously and explore them before proceeding with therapy.
- Make sure there are no heavy movable objects in the office.

the patient's propensity for harm and can ask permission to bring in a potential victim for intervention. Patients usually welcome such efforts on some level because they too wish resolution to the unpleasant and highly charged affair. In some cases, a period of hospitalization allows therapy of the patient and potential victim to proceed or medication to reduce the intensity of the patient's rage.

Long-term therapy allows for the formation of transference. In the case of violent patients, transference can lead to the development of violent ideation directed at the therapist or at other figures on the outside of therapy. The clinician must be attuned to such occurrences, particularly in the case of patients with more primitive character disorders, who may translate feelings for or against the therapist into "acting-out" behaviors at home or in the workplace. Warning victims may be less important than working with the patient to develop an understanding of toward whom the patient is really angry. To put the matter another way, the notification of victims takes place only when insight and introspection fail and the situation cannot be controlled any other way. Collegial consultation may be useful in assessing when the patient is truly dangerous, and when the therapist may be overreacting.

As patients slowly give up becoming violent, a risk of despondency ensues, similar to the phenomenology of the postpsychotic depressive state seen in the long-term therapy of schizophrenic patients. Aggressive patients value being aggressive and to relinquish such behaviors is to be confronted with passivity and dependency, as well as with the helplessness inherent in being weak. This therapeutic task is large, and violent patients, irrespective of etiology, test the clinician's capacity for patience and optimism. Such patients also can evoke within the therapist conflicts about the latter's own aggressions and inhibitions. Forensic psychiatrists are often more comfortable with the handling of dangerous patients and criminals than the clinicians in a more traditional psychiatric practice. An ability on the part of the therapist to discuss one's caseload with colleagues and to subject decisions and problems to peer scrutiny is crucial.

■ REFERENCES

1. Lion JR, Tardiff K: The long-term treatment of the violent patient, in The American Psychiatric Association Annual Review, vol 6. Edited by Hales RE, Frances AJ. Washington, DC, American Psychiatric Press, 1987

2. Tardiff K, Koenigsberg H: A study of assaultive behavior among psychiatric outpatients. Am J Psychiatry 1985; 142:960–963

3. Tardiff K, Sweillam A: Assault, suicide and mental illness. Arch Gen Psychiatry 1980; 37:164–169

4. Tardiff K: Characteristics of assaultive patients in private hospitals. Am J Psychiatry 1984; 141:1232–1239

5. Lion JR, Pasternak SA: Countertransference reactions to violent patients. Am J Psychiatry 1973; 130:207–210

BEHAVIORAL THERAPY 9

Behavioral therapy is an effective but complex and rigorous approach to the management of violent behavior in severely impaired institutional populations. This approach may be used for severely impaired patients (e.g., chronic schizophrenics, mentally retarded patients) in conjunction with other treatment approaches. As will become apparent as one reads this chapter, the general psychiatrist or other mental health professional will not be able to plan and implement the behavioral therapy program but should be in a position to appreciate the benefits of such a program and be able to translate some of these principles into care.

The basic principles outlined in this chapter have been drawn from the work of Liberman and Wong (1) and Wong et al. (2). The basic goal of the behavior treatment program is to convert an unstructured hospital setting, which may promote violent behavior among patients, into a structured setting that will provide stimuli aimed at decreasing violent behavior and increasing prosocial behavior.

■ DEVELOPMENT OF A TREATMENT PLAN

In setting up a behavioral treatment program on an inpatient unit, the services of a trained experienced behavioral analyst should be obtained. It is the responsibility of the behavioral analyst to plan the treatment program in conjunction with the interdisciplinary staff and to train and supervise staff in the implementation of the treatment program. Behavioral treatment programs should be periodically reviewed by persons other than the ward personnel to ensure their quality and ethical standards. In addition, the patient should be involved as much as possible in the formulation of the plan. Informed written consent should be obtained if the patient is competent to do so. The goals and process of the treatment program should be discussed with the patient, and an assessment should be made of the patient's desires in terms of privileges and rewards that may be used to motivate positive behavior.

The first part of the behavioral program should be the specification of target behaviors that will be addressed. These behaviors must be specifically stated. For example, "physical aggression" would be too nonspecific and should be defined more precisely such as "pulling other person's hair, biting, kicking, punching, scratching" and so on. For each target behavior, there should be a clearly specified response by the staff to the behavior.

■ POSITIVE REINFORCEMENT

The first group of behavioral responses or techniques involves positive ways of influencing a patient's behavior. Token economies have been used in institutions for the management of violence as well as to promote basic living skills. Token economy programs are analogous to the monetary system that motivates people in society. Instead of receiving institutional services free of charge, patients are expected to perform at a higher level of functioning to earn tokens that can be exchanged for cigarettes, food, and other privileges. In terms of the management of violence, token economies usually require the patient to go for a certain period of time without physical aggression toward others in order to be promoted to a higher level of the program (i.e., one with more privileges).

In terms of violent patients, often reinforcement for nonviolent behavior must be given in the early phase of treatment at the end of very short intervals (e.g., every few seconds or every few minutes). One type of program is differential reinforcement of other behavior (DRO). This involves delivery of reinforcement following a specific period of time during which inappropriate behavior (e.g., violence) has not occurred. At the end of each time period, which may be in seconds to minutes, a patient receives reinforcement (e.g., praise, attention, food, cigarettes) for the absence of assaultive or destructive behavior. As the program continues, the patient becomes more cooperative, and reinforcement can be spaced out over longer periods of time, eventually resulting in a token economy program.

A variant of this is differential reinforcement of low rate behavior (DRL). This type of program provides positive reinforcement if the rate of violent behavior or other undesirable behavior falls below a particular level (e.g., two violent episodes per hour). The patient would be scheduled to receive reinforcement if aggressive once per hour or less. Another variant is differential reinforcement of incompatible behavior (DRI), which is the administration of positive stimuli for behavior that is physically impossible to perform at the same time as violent behavior. For example, if verbal threats were the target behavior, the DRI schedule would involve the reinforcement for the absence of threats and the presence of positive friendly conversation.

■ TEACHING SOCIAL SKILLS

In conjunction with these positive reinforcement approaches, the patient, once under control, may be taught social skills as alternatives to aggressive and destructive behavior. Clearly disturbed patients may become violent because they are unable to use social skills (e.g., solicitation, persuasion, and negotiation). Behavior therapists may embark on training patients to use these alternatives to violence 1) by giving instructions describing and providing the rationale for the behavior being taught, 2) by modeling or demonstrating the desired behavior, 3) by rehearsing the behavior with the patient, and 4) by giving positive reinforcement for the performance of the correct behavior. Social skills training can teach alternatives to violent behavior, including appropriate affect, facial expressiveness, proper posture, direct eye contact, appropriate expression of frustration, and requests for the listener to change his or her behavior. Success for these social skills learned in the role-playing situation would be translated to the natural setting of the inpatient unit of the ward.

■ NEGATIVE STIMULI

In contrast to the types of programs discussed so far, there are programs that use negative stimuli or the withholding or withdrawing of positive stimuli to decrease violent behavior and other undesirable behaviors. The first type of program is social extinction, which is useful if the aggressive behavior is harmless and does not lead to more serious violent behavior. This approach involves deliberately not responding to the patient's inappropriate behavior by ignoring or turning away from the patient. In this type of program, it is important that all staff be consistent in their responses to the patient's inappropriate behavior.

Another type of approach involves withdrawing positive reinforcement when violent or other inappropriate behavior occurs. This involves the patient losing privileges or being fined in terms of tokens. Thus the patient has less access to grounds privileges, food, and other positive reinforcements. A related program is sensory extinction, where self-injurious behavior is self-stimulatory. For example, a patient banging his head can be fitted with protective helmet and padded gloves to decrease the stimulation from such behavior; a patient who scratches his face may be treated by rubber gloves.

Other programs remove the patient from the environment or treatment program for varying periods of times. Contingent observation removes the patient from participating in an activity for a short period of time following violence or other inappropriate behavior, usually of a minor nature. The patient may be instructed to leave the activity and sit in a chair nearby for a few minutes while watching the appropriate behavior of other patients. After five to 15 minutes of watching others, the patient can rejoin the activity.

Moving to more restrictive procedures is seclusionary time-out or time-out from reinforcement. This involves placing the patient in a special area without any reinforcements following violent or other inappropriate behavior. This may actually involve a seclusion room. Unlike seclusion used for the emergency situations described earlier in this book, seclusionary time-out is administered immediately following display of a specific target behavior, whether it is of immediate danger to others or not. Unlike the use of seclusion in the emergency situation, it is brief, lasting as little as five minutes and rarely longer than one hour. Unlike the emergency use of seclusion, the physician need not see a patient each time he or she is placed in seclusionary time-out. Again, such a plan would receive overall approval and review.

Another more restrictive procedure is contingent restraint, which involves immobilizing some part of a patient's body by some device (e.g., soft ties, restraint chair, cuffs, posey jacket) following the occurrence of a specific violent act. The patient is in time-out from reinforcement, and the staff give no attention to the patient other than what is necessary for medical reasons. Contingent restraint may be preferred to seclusionary time-out if the patient has demonstrated self-injurious behaviors that would occur if left alone in seclusion. One should be cautious that the patient not actually enjoy being restrained or secluded (i.e., as a way of avoiding the activities of the ward and becoming isolated).

TABLE 1. **Elements of Behavioral Treatment**

- Services of trained, experienced behavioral therapist and adequate, trained staff
- Treatment program planned with staff and patient and reviewed by external persons
- Clear definition of target behaviors and the behavioral therapy responses to each
- Behavioral techniques from least to most restrictive:

  1. Positive reinforcement (e.g., token economies; differential reinforcement of other behaviors, low rates of behavior, or other incompatible behavior)
  2. Teaching social skills as alternatives to violence
  3. Withdrawing positive reinforcement or ignoring undesirable behavior
  4. Sensory extinction with physical devices
  5. Contingent observation
  6. Seclusionary time-out and/or contingent restraint

Behavioral treatment programs should be planned and implemented by professionals trained in behavioral therapy. These programs should be reviewed initially and periodically by staff not involved with the patient's direct treatment. The basic elements of behavioral treatment are listed in Table 1.

■ REFERENCES

1. Liberman RP, Wong SE: Behavioral analysis and therapy procedures related to seclusion and restraint, in The Psychiatric Uses of Seclusion and Restraint. Edited by Tardiff K. Washington, DC, American Psychiatric Press, 1984
2. Wong SE, Woolsey JE, Innocent AJ, et al: Behavioral treatment of violent psychiatric patients. Psychiatr Clin North Am 1988; 11:569–580

10 SHORT-TERM PREDICTION OF VIOLENCE

The evaluation of a patient's violence potential is done in the emergency room or in the outpatient office when a decision must be made in terms of whether to admit a patient to a hospital when the clinician has the duty to protect potential victims of one's patients. This evaluation is made also at the time one is considering discharging a patient from the hosptial. The prediction of violent behavior by psychiatrists is a controversial one, with some professionals maintaining that we have no greater expertise in this area than an intelligent layperson. A list of elements forming a decision about short-term potential for violence is in Table 1.

TABLE 1. **Elements Forming a Decision About Short-Term Potential for Violence**

- Information should come from the patient as well as family members, police, other persons, prior clinical records, arrest records, and other legal proceedings.
- Appearance of the patient: signs of alcohol or drug use, agitation, anger, degree of compliance with procedures, or disorganized behavior.
- How detailed or well planned a threat of violence is.
- What are the available means of inflicting serious injury (e.g., purchase or possession of a gun)?
- Past history of violence or other impulsive behaviors: suicide, destruction of property, reckless driving, reckless spending, sexual acting-out, or other antisocial behaviors.
- Target(s) of past violence toward others.
- Degree of injury in violence toward others.
- Circumstances and patterns of escalation of violence toward others.
- History of the patient's physical abuse as a child or occurrence of other familial violence as a child.
- Presence of alcohol or drug use, particularly cocaine, amphetamines, anxiolytics, sedatives, and hallucinogens.
- Presence of other organic disorders including central nervous system as well as other medical disorders affecting the central nervous system.
- Presence of any psychotic psychopathology, particularly paranoid delusions or command hallucinations.
- Presence of organic, borderline, or antisocial personality disorders.
- Being in a demographic group with increased prevalence of violence: young, male, lower socioeconomic groups.
- Written documentation that the information above has been obtained and weighed and how a decision as to whether the patient poses a potential for violence or not has been based on that information.
- Continued assessment of violence potential should be made at short intervals of time (e.g., every few days or a week).

■ ANALOGY TO SUICIDE POTENTIAL

I maintain that a well-trained psychiatrist or other mental health professional should be able to predict a patient's short-term violence potential using assessment techniques analogous to the short-term predictors of suicide potential. Short-term is defined as a period of a few days or a week at most, until the patient is seen for the next therapy session or aftercare or follow-up appointment. Beyond that time, there is an opportunity for many intervening factors, as in the case of the stabilized schizophrenic patient stopping neuroleptic medication or the abstinent spouse abuser resuming drinking. As with prediction of suicide, one focuses on the clinical aspects of the evaluation, namely psychopathology, and must take into consideration demographic, historical, and environmental factors that may be related to an increased risk of violence or suicide.

In making a decision about violence potential, one should interview the patient as well as family members, police, and other persons with information about the patient and violent incidents to guard against the patient minimizing dangerousness. One should review old charts for previous episodes of violence, arrest records, and other records of judicial proceedings if available.

The evaluation of homicide potential is analogous to that of suicide potential. Even if the patient does not express thoughts of violence, one should routinely ask as part of every evaluation the subtle question, "Have you ever lost your temper?" If the answer is yes, then the evaluator should proceed in terms of how, when, and so on in the same manner one would check for suicide potential with, "Have you ever felt that life was not worth living?" If the answer is yes, one would proceed with the evaluation of suicide.

■ APPEARANCE OF THE PATIENT

The appearance of the patient may prompt further scrutiny of the potential for violence. This includes the loud, agitated, angry-appearing patient who is impatient and refuses to comply with the usual intake procedures in the emergency room or clinic as well as the quiet, guarded patient who requires careful listening to for subtle violent ideation. Dysarthria, unsteady gait, dilated pupils, tremors, and other signs of acute drug or alcohol intoxication dictate caution and serious consideration of the patient's potential for violence, even though threats of violence may not be expressed.

■ HOW WELL PLANNED IS THE THREAT?

Along the same lines as the evaluation of suicide potential, evaluation of violence potential includes how well planned the threat is. Vague threats of killing someone are not as serious, all things being equal, to saying, "I'm going to kill my wife because she is having an affair."

■ AVAILABLE MEANS

As with suicide, the availability of a means of inflicting injury is important. For example, if the patient has recently purchased or owns a gun, one should obviously take the threat more seriously. If a weapon can be confiscated, this reduces the potential for homicide.

■ PAST HISTORY OF VIOLENCE OR IMPULSIVITY

A past history of violence or other impulsive behavior is often predictive of future violence. One should ask about injuries to other persons, destruction of property, suicide attempts, reckless driving, reckless spending, criminal offenses, sexual acting-out, and other impulsive behaviors. I have found that violent patients admitted to public hospitals were more likely than nonviolent patients to have a history of prior arrests and violence. Furthermore, a history of prior suicide attempts was found in a greater proportion for violent patients compared to nonviolent patients. Basic research has suggested that suicide and externally directed violence may share the same mechanisms in the brain that produce impulsivity (i.e., low levels of serotonin).

One should assess the degree of past injuries, (e.g., broken bones and lacerations) as well as toward whom violence has been directed and under what circumstances. Often there is a pattern of past violent behavior in specific circumstances (e.g., escalation of a dispute between a husband and wife or parent and child about issues of money, esteem, or sexuality. Unlike suicide, the presence of others at home may not tip the balance toward safety, but rather may increase the propensity toward violence unless the dynamics of past violent episodes are explored and prevented.

A past history of being abused as a child or being in a family where physical abuse occurred should be sought. Being abused as a child is related to becoming a physically abusive adult (i.e., a child abuser or otherwise violent adult). There is evidence that not only is being abused as a child related to adult violence, but witnessing intrafamily violence (e.g., spouse abuse) is related to increased problems with violence. Likewise, a history of obstetrical complications or subsequent head injury should be explored.

■ ALCOHOL AND DRUG USE

Alcohol and drug use should be assessed. Substances that can produce violent behavior include alcohol, barbiturates, other sedatives, and anxiolytic drugs as a result of the intoxicated state as well as during withdrawal. Other substances that can produce violence when the patient is intoxicated include amphetamines and other sympathomimetics, cocaine, phencyclidine (PCP) and other hallucinogens, anticholinergics, and steroids as well as glue sniffing. One should look for dysarthria, nystagmus, unsteady gait, dilated pupils, tachycardia, and tremors, all of which may indicate that a substance abuse disorder is present. Alcohol and drugs are important factors in violence, through the pharmacologic effect of disinhibition, during withdrawal in the case of alcohol and sedatives; or through excitement, disorganization, and delusional thinking in the case of cocaine, amphetamines, and some hallucinogens.

■ OTHER ORGANIC MENTAL DISORDERS

Organicity increases the risk of violence. Central nervous system disorders that have been associated with violent behavior include traumatic brain injuries, intracranial infections (including encephalitis and postencephalitic syndrome), tumors, partial complex seizures, cerebrovascular disorders, Alzheimer's disease, Wilson's disease, multiple sclerosis, and normal pressure hydrocephalus. Some systemic disorders affecting the central nervous system include metabolic disorders (e.g., hypoglycemia), electrolyte imbalances, hypoxia, uremia, Cushing's disease, vitamin deficiencies (e.g., pernicious anemia), systemic infections, systemic lupus erythematosus, porphyria, and industrial poisons (e.g., lead). The assessment and phenomenology of violence resulting from organic disorders are covered in Chapter 6.

■ PSYCHOSIS

As with suicide, the presence of a psychosis should make one take threats of violence very seriously and the assessment of violence potential essential, even if threats are not apparent. The paranoid schizophrenic patient poses a number of problems. First of all, paranoid delusions may not be obvious, or the patient may attempt to hide them. Therefore, the evaluator must listen for subtle clues and should follow up regarding the assessment of violence toward others. Another problem with the violent paranoid schizophrenic patients is noncompliance with medication once they have been stabilized. Other types of schizophrenics have more disorganized symptomatology, and violence may be the result of that or delusional or hallucinatory symptoms, particularly command hallucinations. Manics are also disorganized and less intentional in terms of their violent behavior. Depressed patients are rarely violent; when they are, however, it is usually the case of patients who have psychotic depressions and who murder their spouse and/or children and then commit suicide.

■ PERSONALITY DISORDERS

Personality disorders particularly prone to violence include the explosive (organic) personality and borderline and antisocial personality disorders. With the organic personality or intermittent explosive disorder, there are several discrete episodes of loss of control involving violence toward others or destruction of property. A violent episode may have little apparent precipitating cause or may be linked to predictable patterns of escalation of conflict between the patient and others, usually family members. In any case, violence is out of proportion to any precipitating factor. The violence may occur for a few minutes or an hour and is often associated with alcohol use. It is followed by remorse and feelings of guilt concerning the beating of a spouse or child or other family member. There are a few problems with impulse control or violence between episodes.

This is in contrast to the antisocial personality where there also are intermittent episodes of violent behavior. Between these violent outbursts, there is a pervasive antisocial behavior without remorse and violence on an ongoing basis (e.g., theft, drug dealing, job problems, lying, and reckless driving). Differing from the intermittent explosive disorder, the borderline personality manifests, in addition to episodic violence, a broad instability of interpersonal relationships and profound mood and identity problems. Violence is just one of many impulsive behaviors, others being sexual acting-out, overspending, overeating, suicide attempts, and drug and alcohol abuse.

■ DEMOGRAPHIC CHARACTERISTICS

Demographic characteristics of patients should be considered, with increased risk of violence among the young; males; and persons coming from environments of poverty, disruption of families, and decreased social control, where violence is a more acceptable means of attaining a goal than in other segments of society. I have not found race to be a factor associated with increased risk of assault among psychiatric patients when socioeconomic variables and education are taken into consideration. Rather, the environment from which the patient comes must be considered in the determination of violence potential: is it one that views violence as an accepted means of obtaining what one wants in the face of poverty or lack of other legitimate means, education, work, and verbal skills?

■ SUMMARY

The assessment of violence potential for the short-term (i.e., in days or a week) is analogous to the assessment for suicide potential. The clinician must consider the following:

- Subtle questioning of the patient if violence is not mentioned
- Appearance of the patient
- How well planned a threat of violence is
- Available means of inflicting injury
- Past history of violence and impulsive behavior with attention to frequency, degree of past injuries to others and self, toward whom, and under what circumstances

- Past history of abuse as a child and witnessing domestic violence
- Alcohol and drug use
- Presence of other organic mental disorders
- Presence of certain personality and impulse control disorders
- Demographic characteristics of the patient

All of these factors are weighed in the final assessment of whether the patient poses a significant risk to others so that some action is necessary on the part of the evaluator. Action may include changing the treatment plan, hospitalizing the patient, or warning the intended victim and/or the police. All of the data on which the decision that the patient is or is not a risk for violence *must* be documented in writing; the thinking process through which the decision was made should be evident in the written documentation. Reassessment of violence potential should be made at short intervals (e.g., from visit to visit or every few days) if the patient is to continue to be treated outside of the hospital or other institution. Clinicians have not been faulted for inaccurate prediction but for failure to collect data necessary for the prediction of violence and to use the data logically to make a prediction.

LEGAL ISSUES IN THE MANAGEMENT OF VIOLENT PATIENTS

11

■ BALANCE OF LIBERTY VERSUS PROTECTION OF OTHERS AND THE PATIENT

There are basic ethical concepts that form the legal foundation of the management of the violent patient. Medical ethics, the study of values that are associated with patient care, form the framework for resolving conflicts and values. The central values in the area of violence include the concept of individual autonomy, free will, and freedom to think, feel, and act. One classic proponent of this concept was John Stuart Mill. His philosophy of utilitarianism placed happiness of the individual in the center of the moral arena. A proponent of autonomy was Immanuel Kant, although he differed from Mill in regard to which component of the mind is free. He maintained that it was the thinking rational component rather than the emotional one that was of central concern in the autonomy of the individual.

There is another value, one that conflicts with autonomy: namely, the prevention of harm to the individual and others in society. There are situations in which individual liberty must be limited. Even Mill conceded that the only purpose for which power can be rightfully exercised over a person against his or her will is to prevent harm to others. Although Mill did not see the good of the individual as a sufficient warrant for such deprivation of liberty, a related concept of paternalism does. In other words, we have the responsibility of preventing patients from either directly or indirectly harming themselves.

Thus there is a balance in the ethics of the control of violence. On the one hand are freedom and autonomy of the individual and on the other hand protection of society and the individual from violence. In terms of protection of the individual versus society, there is a further balance of components relevant to the development of clinical guidelines: namely, whether control such as seclusion, restraint, or involuntary medication is used both for the benefit of the patient and others or entirely for the protection of society. There are questions as to whether psychiatrists should be involved with such control if there is no benefit for the patient. Another factor is that of the competence of the individual in terms of his or her protection by paternalistic authorities: whether the individual is an "adult" rather than a "child." This has particular relevance in the area of involuntary medication and informed consent.

In this chapter, I will outline the general legal principles and parameters in the management of violence by psychiatric patients. Although some court decisions may be cited occasionally, this will not be the focus because specific legal parameters may vary among the jurisdictions or institutions in which clinicians practice.

■ INVOLUNTARY HOSPITALIZATION

There are a number of basic principles underlying involuntary hospitalization (civil commitment) (Table 1). Valuable discussion of these is included in the American Psychiatric Association model state law on civil commitment of the mentally ill (1). This model state law recommends that persons can be taken into custody by the police or accepted by the ambulance service and transported to a treatment facility for emergency psychiatric evaluation when a licensed physician certifies, in writing, that he or she has examined the patient in the last 72 hours or has ongoing medical responsibility for the person and, on that basis, has probable cause to believe that the person is suffering from a severe mental disorder as the result of which the individual lacks the capacity to make an informed decision concerning treatment. Furthermore, the physician must certify that the patient 1) is likely to cause harm to the self or to suffer substantial mental or physical deterioration, or 2) is likely to cause harm to others and that immediate hospitalization is necessary to prevent such harm.

At the treatment facility, another psychiatrist would examine the patient. This clinician would determine if the patient

TABLE 1. **Principles of Involuntary Hospitalization**

- Two physicians examine the patient and have reason to believe that the patient:

  1. has a mental disorder;
  2. lacks the capacity to make an informed decision about hospitalization;
  3. is likely to cause harm to self, suffer substantial mental or physical deterioration, or cause harm to others; and
  4. needs immediate hospitalization to prevent such harm.

- The court is asked by the hospital to consider the opinions above within a short time after the patient is involuntarily admitted to the hospital.
- If the court concurs, the patient is held for a period of time (e.g., 30 days); if not, the patient is discharged.
- The court periodically reviews the patient's status and the need for continued hospitalization.

suffers from a severe mental disorder and, as a result, lacks the capacity to make an informed decision concerning treatment and is likely to cause danger to the self, to suffer substantial deterioration, or to cause harm to others.

If the two physicians certify that this is the case, the patient can be admitted to a treatment facility. The patient would receive a preliminary hearing before the court within five business days of admission. If the court concurs with the psychiatrists, then the patient can be held for a 30-day commitment. Otherwise, the patient is discharged. The commitment period may be repeated after a court hearing for 60 days. Then the patient can be recommitted for another 180-day period.

Responses to the model commitment law have been summarized and discussed by Stone (2). Civil libertarians question the ability of one psychiatrist to decide whether a person should be referred for admission and whether that decision will reflect referral to the appropriate institution. They are also concerned about due process and the patient's rights in this procedure. They argue for a high criterion for danger to others (i.e., that one actually perform a violent act toward someone). They argue against the paternalistic criterion for involuntary hospitalization, which says that it should be used only to prevent suffering of the patient and deterioration. Some psychiatrists have expressed their concern that once the patient is admitted, inadequate treatment is the rule because of inadequate funding. Others argue that there should be proper advocacy in the hospital to make certain that the necessary services are delivered and that there is prevention of patient abuse or neglect.

Appelbaum (3) pointed out that since the early 1970s most states have adopted more criminal-like procedures for the evaluation of patients. Many states have adopted formal rules of evidence that require the exclusion of hearsay testimony from commitment hearings. He pointed out that some states require evaluating psychiatrists to warn patients that anything they say may be used to commit them, thus encouraging patients to remain silent during evaluation for admission. Although the adoption of criminal procedures for hearings is intended to protect patients' rights, there is concern that these will further infringe on the psychiatrist's ability to evaluate and treat patients.

Another concern about the model commitment law is that it

is very narrow in terms of requiring a severe degree of mental illness, which in most cases is interpreted as the patient being psychotic. In addition, the provision that the patient should lack the capacity to make an informed decision concerning treatment can be seen as a barrier to the protection of others or the patient in cases where the patient is competent to make treatment decisions but still poses a danger. Informed consent is a key principle, thus, in determination of civil commitment as well as determination of whether the patient should receive involuntary treatment including medication, seclusion, restraint, and other modalities.

■ INFORMED CONSENT

Informed consent is a doctrine that reflects again the value of individual liberty or autonomy: that patients are in control of their own bodies and minds and what is done to them even if the purpose is to help them (Table 2). The roles of the doctor and the patient have been outlined by Lidz et al. (4). The role of psychiatrists in this doctrine is to find out what the problem is, to determine how it can be solved and treated, to consider alternatives, to assess the risk, to explain it to the patient, to get consent, and then to carry out treatment.

The role of the patient is to cooperate and give the psychiatrist valid information and access to his or her body and mind. The patient also has a responsibility to listen to the information from the psychiatrist, to consider it in a logical manner, and to weigh the risk versus the benefits in terms of personal, emotional, and other factors in his or her life. If the patient consents, then the patient is expected to cooperate with the treatment.

Thus informed consent involves information (disclosure) and consent (i.e., the ability to understand information and the capacity for making a rational decision that is voluntary). Yet this process is complex and not well defined. For example, what does the psychiatrist tell the patient; how much does the psychiatrist have to explain of the illness and diagnosis, have to describe details of treatment, and have to describe to what degree the treatment is standard or experimental? How much should the psychiatrist emphasize the benefits as opposed to what the patient can reasonably expect in terms of treatment risks and side effects, and the frequency and severity of these side effects?

TABLE 2. **Principles of Informed Consent**

Role of the physician:
1. Find out what the problem is
2. Find out how it can be treated
3. Consider alternatives in terms of benefits and risks to the patient
4. Explain the problem, treatment, and risks and benefits to the patient
5. Get consent from the patient
6. Carry out the treatment

Role of the patient:
1. Give valid information and access to one's body
2. Listen to the information the physician provides
3. Consider the information in a logical, rational manner
4. Consider the risks versus the benefits in terms of personal factors in his or her life
5. Consent if the patient wants to do so
6. Cooperate with treatment if consent is given

Exceptions to these principles:
1. In emergencies when there is no time for the physician and patient to fulfill these roles
2. When the patient is not competent to fulfill his or her role at the time a decision about treatment is to be made

Who gives consent in these exceptions:
1. In emergencies, the doctor and treatment team decide about treatment
2. In other situations, the family and close friends, or the court

How much information the psychiatrist should give the patient has been debated. Most would agree that a psychiatrist need not tell the patient everything about treatment of the disease because the amount and complexity of the information would be too much for lay patients. If not everything is told to the patient, there are differing views about what should be told. One side says that the doctor should tell the patient what most doctors would tell patients about the illness, treatment, risk, and benefits. The other side argues that the doctor should tell the patient what a reasonable layperson or consumer would need to make an informed decision about treatment. This debate has not been resolved.

There are other issues about disclosure. For example, when should a patient be told information? How should a patient be told information (e.g., by writing, by videotape)? Does the psychiatrist describe the procedure and medication in a matter of fact manner so that the patient does not take it seriously or is the doctor overly persuasive or authoritarian, leaving no room for questions or doubts from the patient?

There are two exceptions to informed consent that are relevant for the management of violent patients. The first is treatment in an emergency when there is no time for informed consent, for adequate disclosure, or for the patient to decide. This can be illustrated in terms of the violent patient who is in the midst of being violent or is imminently violent toward others. The second exception is that of incompetency. In this case, there is a question of the patient's capacity to understand the information given by the psychiatrist in terms of the nature of the illness, nature of the treatment, benefits and risks, and alternatives. The patient is unable to make a reasonable, rational decision about treatment. It may be possible for a patient to be involuntarily hospitalized but yet still be able to participate in informed consent (i.e., to understand and to make a decision about treatment). The key point is understanding and making a rational choice at the time of decision.

In general, if the patient lacks the capacity for informed consent and is incompetent, in emergencies the doctor and the treatment team make the decision. If in non-emergency situations, family members closest to the patient may make decisions about treatment. More frequently, there are judicial or administrative mechanisms to decide whether 1) the patient lacks the capacity to make a decision, and 2) if a patient did have the capacity, what would the decision be in terms of treatment.

■ INVOLUNTARY TREATMENT AND THE RIGHT TO REFUSE TREATMENT

The ability to hospitalize a patient involuntarily is separate from the legal ability of a psychiatrist to treat the patient involuntarily. This poses a number of problems. These problems arise most notably with the administration of medication (Table 3), particularly neuroleptics. The ability of a patient to give informed consent is also relevant for the use of behavioral treatment approaches for the management of violence. Appelbaum (5) pre-

TABLE 3. **Refusal of Medication by a Patient**

1. In emergencies when there is danger of harm to self or others, the physician can make the decision to give involuntary medication.
2. In other situations, the reason for refusal must be determined.
3. If the patient is incompetent, procedures differ by jurisdictions:
   A. independent review and approval of involuntary medication is made by health professionals not involved with the patient's daily treatment, or
   B. judicial review of the patient's competency and substituted judgment by the courts determines treatment.
4. If the patient is competent, the clinician should assess why the patient refuses medication:
   A. the patient has not received enough information,
   B. there are cultural or religious beliefs as grounds for refusal,
   C. there is pressure from family or other significant persons in the patient's life, or
   D. events or dynamics on the ward have influenced the patient's refusal.

sented differing models in terms of right to refuse treatment. He pointed out that the legal right to refuse neuroleptic medication is now more than a decade old, beginning with a series of decisions in the *Rogers* case in Massachusetts. He pointed out that judicial decisions on the right to refuse treatment have fallen into two types: treatment-driven and rights-driven. The treatment-driven model defers to the physician's decision in terms of whether medication is appropriate even if the patient refuses medication. In many state jurisdictions there are provisions for independent clinical reviews of the appropriateness of the medication, usually by professionals not involved with the patient's daily care. The basic principle is that of professionals' responsibility for caring for patients balances that of individual autonomy.

The rights-driven model reaffirms the individual's rights to liberty and to control intrusions on his or her body. In this model, judicial reviews of the patient's competency, the appropriateness of the medication, and the patient's best interest if the patient is incompetent are the focus. Increasingly, this has become the model long-standing in Massachusetts and, more recently, in New York. An interesting way of making incompetency determination not an issue is that of the model commitment law where only patients who are incompetent and who meet the other criteria can be admitted against their will. This ensures that all patients who are committed are incompetent; then the issue is merely appropriateness of treatment in the context of substituted judgment for the patient.

In emergencies, the clinician is on sound ground and the patient is involuntarily medicated to prevent injury to the self or others. In the non-emergency situation, Wettstein (6) gave clinical advice about how to proceed. The clinician should assess why the patient is refusing medication or other treatment. The competence of the patient to give informed consent as has been outlined earlier should be assessed by the clinician. If the patient is incompetent, then in most jurisdictions judicial-type proceedings in terms of substituted judgment would be appropriate.

If the patient is competent to refuse medication, the reasons for the refusal should be assessed. The patient may not understand the benefits versus the risk of treatment, may be denying the severity of the illness or violence potential, or may have cultural or religious grounds for refusal of medication. As has been pointed out in the use of seclusion and restraint, one should also assess the dynamics of the ward environment or, if the patient is an outpatient, the dynamics of the family and other significant persons in that patient's life. The clinician should attempt to rectify any problems or reasons for refusing medication in a competent patient.

■ SECLUSION AND RESTRAINT

Wexler (7) summarized the legal aspects of seclusion and restraint in the emergency situation as well as the use of seclusion- and restraint-like procedures in behavioral treatment of violent patients (Table 4). The most important court decision governing the use of seclusion and restraint is that of the U.S. Supreme Court decision of *Youngberg v Romeo* (8). In this decision, the Supreme Court acknowledged the patient's right to liberty, but indicated that this should be balanced by the institution's duty to protect the patient and others from acts of violence. In deciding whether the patient should be deprived of liberty (i.e., secluded or restrained), the Court deferred to clinical judgment in that courts should make certain that professional judgment was exercised.

TABLE 4. **Legal Principles in Seclusion and Restraint**

1. Courts have deferred to decisions by professionals if they follow accepted clinical standards.
2. In emergencies or imminent emergencies, professionals have flexibility in the use of seclusion or restraint based on the specific, individual clinical situation.
3. Liability for injuries to patients can be imposed if clinical standards as to indications, contraindications, assessment, monitoring, and care for patients in seclusion or restraint are not followed.
4. Restrictive seclusion- or restraint-like procedures used in behavioral therapy are sanctioned if they are used to control severe, dangerous behaviors.
5. Restrictive seclusion- or restraint-like procedures used in behavioral therapy are probably not sanctioned if they are used after dangerous behavior has subsided and the patient does not pose an imminent danger to self or others.

The Court indicated that in the seclusion or restraint of a patient, "the decision if made by a professional is presumably valid" and "liability may be imposed only when the decision by a professional is such a substantial departure from accepted professional judgment, practice or standard as to demonstrate the person responsible actually did not base the decision on such a judgment." Appelbaum (5) noted that the Court has rendered a decision only for seclusion and restraint and not for the use of involuntary medication, where it has remanded such decisions to the local and state courts. Thus in the use of seclusion and restraint, the states have not had the privilege of determining whether competency should be the criterion for the non-emergency use of seclusion and restraint (e.g., in cases of escalating agitation and aggression or in cases of the use of seclusion- and restraint-like procedures for behavior treatment).

Wexler (7) pointed out that the clinician has substantial flexibility in the use of seclusion and restraint in emergency situations. In fact, even in imminent physical violence or escalating aggression, most decisions to use seclusion or restraint, if properly documented, can be supported. This calls attention to the need for the clinician and institution to be familiar with the minimal standards proposed by the American Psychiatric Association Task Force on Seclusion and Restraint, as has been outlined in Chapter 4 (9). With adherence to these guidelines for indications, contraindications, assessment by physician, monitoring, and care of the patient in seclusion and restraint, the clinician can be confident that liability will not be imposed even if a patient is inadvertently injured or even killed during these procedures.

In terms of the use of seclusion and restraint for behavior therapy, Wexler (7) made the following observations. In cases where restrictive behavioral techniques (e.g., time-out, restraint) are used as part of a behavioral treatment program, these are usually applied in response to severe, dangerous, disruptive, or destructive behavior. Thus this is supported under *Romeo*'s principles of emergency management in the use of seclusion and restraint. If restrictive procedures are used after the violence has occurred, where the patient does not pose a substantial danger, then the emergency rationale would not apply. Use of seclusion or restraint in these cases would then raise the question of informed consent, the ability of a patient to give it, and presumably the patient's ability, if competent, to withdraw informed consent at any time.

Thus the legal support for the use of seclusion and restraint based on the clinician's decision is stronger than that for involuntary medication and other forms of involuntary treatment.

■ THE CLINICIAN'S DUTY TO PROTECT OTHERS

The physician or other therapist has legal as well as ethical duty to protect intended victims from violence from patients if there exists a professional relationship with the patient (Table 5). The depth of this relationship is not as important as the fact that the relationship exists. For example, a clinician may be very involved with a patient's treatment, as in the case of treatment on an inpatient unit or in outpatient psychotherapy. On the other hand, the relationship may not be as intense, as in the case of providing medical coverage or prescribing medication for patients treated by nonmedical therapists.

Although physicians have always had an ethical duty to protect others, the legal precedent for the duty to protect began with the *Tarasoff* decision in California more than a decade ago. Mr. Poddar was an Indian graduate student at the University of

TABLE 5. **Duty to Protect Intended Victims**

- In most states, the duty of therapists is to protect and not necessarily to warn intended victims of violence by their patients.

- This applies to a patient during evaluation as well as any degree of professional relationship with the therapist in treatment.

- There are three steps in fulfilling the duty to protect:

1. Gather information (see Chapter 6), make a decision about short-term potential for violence (see Chapter 10), and consider consultation with colleague(s).
2. If the patient is a danger, consider alternative plans to protect the victim, select one or more, and give reasons, for example:
   - intensify therapy (e.g., increase frequency of visits),
   - institute a change in medication,
   - involve family to control patient and/or to prevent access to weapons,
   - inform the police,
   - hospitalize the patient or attempt to commit through legal processes, and/or
   - warn intended victim after discussing and considering alternatives with the patient.
3. Implement plan(s) appropriately and effectively in a timely manner and monitor.

California at Berkeley. There he met Ms. Tarasoff. After a brief superficial relationship with him, Ms. Tarasoff ended the relationship. Mr. Poddar was very distraught and was seen and treated in outpatient psychotherapy at the University of California. He told his therapist that he had thoughts of killing Ms. Tarasoff, and the therapist was also told by a friend of the patient that he had purchased a gun. The therapist and his supervisor decided that Mr. Poddar posed a danger to Ms. Tarasoff and decided to hospitalize him. They contacted the university police for assistance in hospitalizing him. The university police spoke to Mr. Poddar, who denied any homicidal ideation. No further action was taken. When Ms. Tarasoff returned from a trip out of the country, Mr. Poddar murdered her.

Her parents sued the University of California for negligence in not confining Mr. Poddar and warning Ms. Tarasoff of Mr. Poddar's threats. The California Supreme Court ruled that the therapist should have warned the intended victim. The psychiatric profession was very concerned that this would pose a broad threat to patient confidentiality. The state supreme court agreed to hear the case again and then decided that the duty of a professional is to protect and not necessarily to warn an intended victim of violence. In most states, this is considered the responsibility of the clinician: to protect and not necessarily to warn an intended victim. Ironically, the state of California has recently passed a law that requires clinicians to warn rather than only to protect intended victims.

Somewhat reassuring, in a review with an excellent presentation of cases from recent court decisions, Beck (10) indicated that most cases have been decided in favor of the defendant (i.e., the clinician). A few cases decided in favor of the plaintiff have appeared, in retrospect, not to have been completely justified. These cases have involved failure of one clinician to communicate a history of violence to a subsequent clinician or a failure of a clinician to obtain past records that indicated that a patient had a history of violence and might be a danger in the future. Another case involving release of a patient who subsequently killed his mother was decided against the defendants because a note was found at home in which the patient threatened to kill his mother. In light of the other proper care in this case, this appears to be a somewhat questionable reason for imposing liability on the defendants. In another case involving release of an inpatient, the clinicians were held liable for not keeping a patient who abused phencyclidine longer in the hospital because of a history of violence despite the fact there were no grounds that justified continued commitment of the patient. In retrospect, the hospital should have petitioned the courts and thus shifted the responsibility for continued hospitalization or discharge to the community into the legal system. Another approach, taken in a successful defense of a clinician in the case of a patient with a history of alcohol abuse, was to document clearly that the clinician made strong efforts to convince the patient prior to discharge not to drink and drive.

Appelbaum (11) presented a three-part model of how the clinician can satisfy the *Tarasoff* obligation to protect intended victims from violence by one's patients. The first stage, that of assessment, has two components. The therapist must gather data relevant to an evaluation of dangerousness and a determination of dangerousness must be made on the basis of that data. In Chapter

6 I have discussed the data I believe necessary for the determination of a patient's violence potential. This includes information on past history of violence, including frequency, victims, and severity, as well as a history of other impulsive behaviors. This information should be sought not only from the patient but also the patient's family, the police, and prior clinical or criminal records. Information should be sought about the patient's developmental history and medical history, including alcohol and substance abuse and other illnesses related to violence. The clinician should assess in-depth and record the patient's mental status, physical status, and any relevant laboratory results, particularly reflecting alcohol or drug abuse. In terms of making a decision about violence potential, I have presented in Chapter 10 a model for the short-term prediction of violence analogous to the assessment of suicide potential. This involves using the data collected and assessing how well planned a threat of violence is; available means of inflicting injury; past history of violence and other impulsive behavior, giving serious weight to any alcohol or drug use; and the presence of organic mental disorders, certain personality and impulse control disorders, and psychosis.

The second part of Appelbaum's (11) model involves selecting a course of action if the clinician decides that the patient poses a serious threat of violence. Although the law has usually restricted the clinician's responsibility for protection of identified victims, in the case of unidentified victims, the clinician should seriously consider commiting or attempting to commit any patient who is deemed a serious risk of violence. This is the best way to protect an unnamed victim, as in the case of a paranoid schizophrenic who has threatened to kill police. Even if the clinician's attempts to commit the patient are unsuccessful, the shifting of responsibility to the legal system is a strategy of risk management.

There is a wide range of alternatives the clinician may consider to protect intended victims short of warning the intended victims. The clinician may decide to intensify treatment by increasing the number of visits or by instituting or increasing medication, particularly in the case of psychotic patients and neuroleptic medication. The clinician may decide to increase compliance by the use of depot neuroleptic medications. The clinician may decide to involve the family in efforts to control the patient or to prevent access to weapons. The clinician may decide to consult with a colleague about the patient's dangerousness and alternatives to control the patient. The clinician may decide to get more information on past violence by the patient. Police may be warned about the patient's threat to the intended victim. If the clinician decides to warn the intended victim, it is not advisable to do this unilaterally in an insensitive way, as did one clinician who lost as a defendant when a letter was sent to a patient's employer warning that the patient had spoken of violence toward him. Instead, it is important to involve the patient in decision making. For example, the patient may be presented with alternatives to warning the intended victim. If the victim is to be warned, it may be advisable to have the patient listen while the clinician discusses the situation with the intended victim. Further, it may be advisable to bring the victim into treatment if the victim is an intimate of the patient and/or a family member.

Once the decision has been made that a patient is dangerous and a plan of action has been formulated, the third part of Appelbaum's model requires the therapists to implement their plan appropriately, in an effective and timely manner. Furthermore, a therapist must continue to monitor the course of action taken, particularly if it does not involve warning the victim or hospitalizing the patient.

All of these efforts will not protect the clinician against liability in cases where the patient is injured or killed if this process is not documented in detail in the patient's record.

■ REFERENCES

1. Stromberg CD, Stone AA: A model state law on civil commitment of the mentally ill. Harvard Journal of Legislation 1983; 20:275–396
2. Stone AA: A response to comments on APA's model commitment law. Hosp Community Psychiatry 1985; 36:984–989
3. Appelbaum PS: Legal aspects of violence by psychiatric patients, in APA Annual Review, vol. 6. Edited by Hales RE, Frances AJ. Washington, DC, American Psychiatric Press, 1987
4. Lidz CW, Meisel A, Zerubavel E: Informed Consent: A Study of Decisionmaking in Psychiatry. New York, Guilford Press, 1984
5. Appelbaum PS: The right to refuse treatment with antipsychotic

medication: retrospect and prospect. Am J Psychiatry 1988; 145:413–419

6. Wettstein RW: Psychiatry and the law, in The American Psychiatric Press Textbook of Psychiatry. Edited by Talbott JA, Hales RE, Yudofsky SC. Washington, DC, American Psychiatric Press, 1988

7. Wexler DB: Legal aspects of seclusion and restraint, in The Psychiatric Uses of Seclusion and Restraint. Edited by Tardiff K. Washington, DC, American Psychiatric Press, 1984

8. *Youngberg v. Romeo*, 102 Supreme Ct 2452 (1982)

9. Tardiff K (ed): The Psychiatric Uses of Seclusion and Restraint. Washington, DC, American Psychiatric Press, 1984

10. Beck JC: The therapist's legal duty when the patient may be violent. Psychiatr Clin North Am 1988; 11:665–679

11. Appelbaum PS: Tarasoff and the clinician: problems in fulfilling the duty to protect. Am J Psychiatry 1985; 142:425–429

INDEX

122